The SECRET WITHIN

No-Nonsense Spirituality for the Curious Soul

ANNEMARIE POSTMA

WATKINS PUBLISHING

LONDON

We are here to actually see what's here to be seen. Hear what's here to be heard. Taste what's here to be tasted. Smell what's here to be smelled. Touch what's here to be touched. And know what's here to be known. ... There's no great mystery to it. There's nothing magical or mysterious or airy-fairy or even spiritual about it in the way that people usually use the word 'spiritual' ...

— JON KABAT-ZINN

Annemarie Postma was born in the Netherlands in 1969. Partially paralysed as a result of an untreated tick bite in childhood, she studied law, but became the first professional model in Europe with a disability, appearing in *Playboy* in 1995. In demand on TV talk shows at home and internationally, she has since become a well-known campaigner and writer with a special interest in self-esteem and self-respect. Since 2005, Annemarie has been goodwill ambassador of the Dutch Foundation for the Disabled Child. She has written several books, including the highly successful *The Deeper Secret*.

This edition first published in the UK and USA 2011 by
Watkins Publishing, Sixth Floor, Castle House,
75–76 Wells Street, London W1T 3QH

1 3 5 7 9 10 8 6 4 2

Designed and typeset by Clare Thorpe

Printed and bound by Imago in China
British Library Cataloguing-in-Publication Data Available
Library of Congress Cataloging-in-Publication Data Available
ISBN: 978-1-907486-50-0

www.watkinspublishing.co.uk

Distributed in the USA and Canada by
Sterling Publishing Co., Inc. 387 Park Avenue South,
New York, NY 10016-8810

For information about custom editions, special sales, premium and
corporate purchases, please contact Sterling Special Sales Department at
800-805-5489 or specialsales@sterlingpub.com

FOREWORD

— TULKU LAMA LOBSANG

We come to this earth to remember who we are. We don't come here to become 'something special', but for insight and self-realization. As soon as you truly know who you are, you are Buddha, you are enlightened. Our biggest assignment in life is to become who we truly are. This means we have to find the silence within us. Inside this silence is our true nature. Truly connecting with this silence – *that* is spirituality.

Many people feel lost and feel as if something is missing in their lives. This is directly connected to their 'dream'. They dream of something that does not actually exist in reality and then lose themselves in it. They hope that someone else or something outside of themselves will bring them true happiness. But in reality this isn't possible, and time and time again they will be left feeling disappointed and dissatisfied.

Happiness is not something we can find outside of ourselves. *We* are happiness. People are very afraid to accept this as the truth, because it means we have to take full responsibility for our own actions. Yet it is the only way to a fulfilling and happy life. As long as we do not take responsibility for ourselves, it is impossible to be truly present and give our complete, undivided attention to the reality of the here and now. Without taking responsibility for our own actions, it is impossible to see that what we seek is already here within us and present in our lives. Instead, life feels as if we are lost in the desert, where you keep walking and walking without ever getting anywhere.

◆

We are not on earth to become 'something special',
but to become ourselves.

◆

Many of us think being 'spiritual' is something extraordinary. In my eyes, being spiritual actually means being no more and no less than just yourself. That what you say, you will do; that your words actually become your deeds; and that you live by what you know. *This* is true spirituality.

Some people seem to know it all and can tell you exactly what is 'right' and 'wrong', yet they don't practise what they preach. In Buddhism we call these people *Dharma ghosts* or *spiritual ghosts*. They know the teachings of Buddha, but don't apply the lessons to their own lives. So it is what we call a 'dead lesson' for them.

When Westerners practise Buddhism, it seems they are doing so in a state of 'laziness'. Laziness is the first blockage for spiritual growth. Most people lack discipline; many people are too lazy for just about everything in life – even too lazy to be happy. Of course it's true that in these modern times we are all incredibly busy with so many obligations. My experience, however, has shown me that the busier I am, the more time I actually have to practise my spiritual exercises. It sounds like a contradiction, but it is true.

The fact that we are so busy doesn't mean that we can't find the time for a moment of silence or an exercise. It is just the opposite: the more time you have on your hands, the less you are bound to accomplish and the more you will put things off. Too much free time actually makes for a chaotic and disorderly life and makes us miss key moments and let important chances for growth pass us by. Also, if you are exceptionally busy, you will realize that you won't have any time left over later, so you will be forced to do the task at hand and finish right away.

Problems are absolutely unavoidable in life. This is entirely a good thing, because problems teach us how to grow. Every new problem is the perfect teacher. You and your problem may not become the best of friends, but it *is* a very useful teacher. Everyday life, with all its blows, offers us a real chance to come to terms with and even reconcile with reality. Only when we no longer fear reality, no longer criticize, fight or try to escape it, do we have a real opportunity to learn and to grow.

Reading about the experiences of others can also help us achieve this, especially if they are written from a present-day point of view and in contemporary language suited to the times we live in. Reading about and listening to the experiences of others is very important. Together with your own experiences, this opens the door to self-knowledge and consciousness. Words and experiences are like a mother and child separated for a long time. When they are finally reunited, they can become *one* again. With all great wisdom the same rule applies: Words together with experience are the key to more wisdom in life.

◆

Annemarie Postma shows us a simple and practical way to live a genuine and fulfilling life.

◆

Annemarie Postma wrote this book from her own experience and unique vision. In the first place, it makes this book a very human book. It is suitable for anyone: 'spiritual beginners' as well as the 'spiritually advanced'.

She truly understands that to be spiritual we do not need to do or be anything exceptional, but that living a spiritual life essentially means letting go of our resistance to reality. This is her message. By always wanting things to be different than they are in reality, we block the road to connecting with our true nature and we stagnate our inner growth.

I absolutely agree that in order to grow we must embrace life exactly as it is today and reconcile with our own humanity. This is not an easy task, but in this book Annemarie Postma reminds us of who we really are and shows us a simple and practical way to live a genuinely spiritual and fulfilling life.

Genuine spiritual teachers teach us something without wanting to change our beliefs. They are not out to force their reality upon others, only to remind them of the power, strength and wisdom within themselves. They share this knowledge, which can be applied by all in their own way, depending on who they are at that very moment. This is the true mark of a spiritual teacher, and Annemarie Postma proves she is exactly this kind of teacher with this book.

This is why this book is of great value to our generation. It speaks to us in a voice we recognize and shows us how we can apply these teachings in our everyday lives. It enriches our spiritual wisdom in a very clear, practical and down-to-earth manner. This is a book for everyone and anyone who wants to make spirituality a part of his or her regular everyday life.

— TULKU LAMA LOBSANG
   TIBETAN DOCTOR AND TEACHER OF BUDDHISM

SPIRITUALITY IS ROOTED IN THE REALITY OF EVERYDAY LIFE

*W*hat exactly is spirituality? What do you get out of living a spiritual life, and how do you apply it to your daily routine? That is precisely what this book is all about.

We live in a tumultuous time of great changes and shifting consciousness. A time with an unprecedented amount of outside influences, choices, distractions and pure chaos. A time in which we as Westerners are trained to hoard, collect and *have* everything we want now so that one day, in some faraway future, we can finally *be*.

Most of us are stuck in 'survival mode': a pattern in which there is very little room to be who you really are and certainly no time to listen to the little voice inside you whispering the true desires of your soul. Living a spiritual life often seems like a luxury for people with extra time and money on their hands. Or an escape for vaguely 'New Agey' people who dive into the world of spirituality because they aren't strong enough to face up to their own reality.

This is all nonsense.

A spiritual life is not something we have to make time for or something we have to find in the outside world somewhere. Life without spirituality simply does not exist, because we are all spiritual beings. Besides, true spirituality isn't something vague, but practical and deeply rooted in the reality of every day. It is not a luxury but a necessity in a world where, now more than ever, we are constantly confronted by the harm that can come to us when spiritual consciousness is lacking.

•

Living a spiritual life often seems like a luxury
or an escape. This is nonsense.

•

Many of us are hungry for real answers to hidden or long-forgotten questions. *Why do I exist and where am I going? How can I give more purpose, meaning and lustre to my life? How do I deal with the stress of my daily life and yet keep my spiritual life in sync? How do I live a spiritual life amid the chaos of every day?*

These are essential questions for curious souls to ask in a time when we are all in desperate need of 'the next step', a step to take us deeper. Not to become preoccupied with self, but to be someone who, with a deeper consciousness, can experience life on a deeper level and become a happier, stronger human being. A person who can engage in more balanced relationships with others, and who, through a real connection with himself or herself, can connect with others – as well as with all things living and all that *is*.

Spirituality changes how you look at things and makes room for expanding your experience. If you start to look at things differently, you will certainly see a whole new world. But you aren't creating changes outside of yourself – you're creating changes inside of yourself, which then change your relationship with everything happening around you. The secret to a spiritual life isn't somewhere 'out there' – it lies within.

Questions for a Curious Soul

Often we ask ourselves in this instant-gratification world we live in: *How can I change something about this situation or about my life?* However, much more interesting questions would actually be: *How do I allow reality in without judgement? How do I come to accept everything as it is? How can I best prepare myself for challenging situations? How can I change the views, thoughts and convictions with which I keep myself imprisoned in a certain reality?*

Is this difficult? Absolutely! If it were easy, we'd all be doing it. Spirituality certainly sounds inviting, but as much as people would like it, it doesn't appear out of thin air. It doesn't come from just wanting it, or even from talking about it. Or from taking an evening class, going on a mindfulness retreat, wearing particular beads, tying a red string around your wrist or following the latest guru.

•

Spirituality is something you do,
but not something you're ever done with.

•

It begins with a simple willingness and comes to you slowly, with time. You'll be falling down and, with discipline and practice, getting up again. I am not a cynic or sceptic, but I am 'spiritually critical': I only believe in real hands-on spirituality, and I know that there is no real spirituality without real discipline. I am a Taurus, and so I am a practical human being. I believe in knowing, thinking and feeling, but especially in *doing*!

So this isn't your typical sit-back-and-read kind of book, but more a go-out-and-do book. Of course I am sharing my own experiences and personal views of life. But in the end, what matters is whether certain insights and ideas inspire *you* to apply them to your daily routine. So as you read, feel and see what speaks to you and what will actually work for you.

This is a book to constantly take small bits and pieces from, going purely on your gut feeling. At night (or any other quiet moment of the day), close your eyes and open the book to any page. You stand a good chance that the paragraph you land on is about exactly what you need to know at that very moment, exactly what you need to be reminded of. While you are reading, stop every now and then and try, without any judgement, to let what you are reading *in*. Take a deep breath here and there, stop when you feel you are 'full' and continue reading only when there is space on your personal hard drive for more input.

All my books come from the core of my being. Just like you, I am on a journey, a spiritual being coming to terms with her humanity while trying to gain inner freedom within all the limitations of our earthly existence.

I draw on my deepest experiences and my own life lessons, offering them only as mirrors for those who want to get to know themselves.

My books are answers to questions I ask myself. They are part of my own personal development and evolution. When I start a new book these days, I have learned that it means that I am entering a new phase in my life and a period of transformation.

What I choose to write about is what I am trying to figure out myself at that time. So in essence the books choose me. What I am doing with my books is reporting live from my own inner journey and sharing new insights I've picked up along the way – sometimes while crawling, sometimes while skipping and quite often while stumbling.

The keys to practical spirituality in this book come from my own life, from what I have studied, learned and experienced; they have opened the window through which I view my life. But this doesn't mean that *I* am the only road to wisdom. Who can claim to be an expert on the human experience? What I am sharing with you is fundamental, but not finished; there is always more to say on this subject.

Each chapter, in fact, could be a whole book on its own. But this is exactly what I am trying to stay away from: endless chatter about spirituality. A spiritual life is about being conscious, awake, responsible and involved in living, with great love, passion and gratitude for life. It is something you do, but not something you can ever be done with: there is no such thing as being 'spiritual' without a real, ongoing investment. As long as we live, we have a lot to do; we have a lot to do *together*. If I have one hope, it is that you are convinced of this after reading this book.

Chapter 1

SPIRITUALITY IS BEING A COMPLETE HUMAN BEING

'What is the path?'
the Zen master Nan-Sen was asked.
He answered:
'Your daily life is the path.'

*S*pirituality. Everyone is talking about it or claiming to practise it. Yet no one can explain properly what living a true spiritual life really means. Often when I meet people who are 'spiritual', I notice their huge need to escape from reality and from their own responsibility – and, last but not least, their total lack of a sense of humour, especially about themselves. They are constantly concerned with the 'proper' way to act, silly rules and even dress codes. It's as if spirituality is more a trendy lifestyle than a very real inner way of life. It's become a way of life that's for sale, offered to you pre-packaged and ready to go. Travelling on your own authentic personal journey is not really required. There are glossy spiritual magazines, books, DVDs, workshops and retreats in exotic places that promise to show us how 'it' is done. Mostly, however, they show us how living a spiritual life *looks* from the outside.

Suddenly spirituality is hip and trendy. It's a way to pass time, something you can pull out of your hat and talk about at parties. It even gives you a certain status –

namely, that of someone who lives consciously and is devoted to personal growth. It suggests profound depth and ethical ideals. *Look at me and how incredibly spiritual I am, I meditate!* It seems that these days everyone is meditating, too. As a matter of fact, if you aren't, you are considered so 'five minutes ago' – passé.

Westerners use meditation mainly to relax and to lower their stress level. But did you know this is not what meditation is actually for at all? Meditation is not a tool from the how-to-drag-yourself-through-life survival kit. It's not meant to help you to simply sustain your life, as if you were treading water, but to give a much deeper meaning to it. It is designed for you to make contact with the real you and fuse together your inner self with your destination in this life.

•

Maybe we should start to think of a new word for spirituality. The true meaning of the word has been lost.

•

Meditation isn't about wearing the proper Ibiza tunic and matching slippers, or jumping into lotus position to *not want* and *not think* with great determination. It is nothing more than doing what you already do, in the purest way possible, with your complete, undivided attention, being completely present in the moment – wherever that may be. It doesn't mean *thinking*, but simply *being*.

It demands your complete attention to the here and now and the place where your physical body is. So meditation can also mean losing yourself completely in cleaning your house, putting all your love and devotion into cooking a nice dinner, or daydreaming while cutting wood. Robin, my significant other, can easily spend an entire evening, with total dedication, fiddling intently with the settings on the computer, the phone or a TV connection to get them 'just right'. When he finally finishes, he feels totally refreshed. It works for him.

At Home in Yourself

Maybe we should start to think of a new word for spirituality. The true meaning of the word has been lost; instead, it's become commonplace, a household word yet full of inaccuracies and loaded with misunderstandings. As if spirituality is something you have to move mountains for and can only achieve in mysterious faraway places. In an old newsletter, I came across a quote from the teacher Sathya Sai Baba, who said, 'These days everyone seems to be looking for godliness. Why would it be necessary to search for something which is already always present everywhere? Do you go search for yourself in the outside world? Someone who would do that is a fool, because what you are doing is distancing yourself from your higher Self and then going to search for it outside of yourself. With such a foolish search party you will waste precious time and get nowhere. All spiritual exercises become obsolete for those who can clearly see that what you seek does not come from anywhere else and is not going anywhere. It doesn't come and it doesn't go, because it's always present within you.'

Often, when I speak with my Tibetan teacher, Lama Lobsang, I think he must be having a great big laugh on the inside when he sees what we all go through in order to 'find ourselves'! Do the Tibetans go away somewhere to become more 'spiritual'? It is the Buddhists themselves who say, 'Wherever you go in the world, your own shadow will follow; you can never escape yourself.' During one of my conversations with the lama, he said, 'I often meet Westerners who tell me they want to become Buddhist monks. My answer is always, "No, that is not necessary if you want to practise Buddhism. Just like my Tibetan outfit doesn't make me a better Buddhist. Many of us are inclined to look elsewhere, to escape. But right here in this spot and inside you, heaven and hell exist together. Heaven is not somewhere else; hell is our own fear."'

This has been my experience as well. You can find that feeling of inner peace and quiet right in your own kitchen while you're cooking dinner, in the woods while you walk your dog and even (or maybe especially) during the most difficult moments in your life. When I look back at my own life's journey, I see that it was the moments of the greatest stress and most extreme grief that offered me the deepest and most loving sense of acceptance, allowed me to surrender in complete devotion and gave me true inner peace. There was no need for me to go anywhere else but where I already was in order to achieve this. During my youth it took place in my little room in the rehabilitation centre or the small hospital rooms where I lay for long periods of time. Later in life, it took place in those same beds where I was effectively 'chained'.

•

There is no need for you to be someone else,
or you would be someone else, right?

•

For example, during my last hospital stay, I had to lie on my right side for seven months straight because of a bedsore on my left thigh and a wound on my left foot. What I remember the most clearly from this period is: total inner peace. There was nothing else I could do but just lie there, so that is what I did. Resisting was not an option; all I could do was surrender to the situation. That hospital room became my sanctuary. The all-important *want this* and *must do that* gave way to acceptance and surrender. My world had become very small, but clear and serenely calm.

There were weeks while I battled a severe case of blood poisoning when I was physically in such a bad state that I could feel how thin the line was between 'here' and 'there'. Still, these recurring moments have always brought me closer to my true nature. Sure, I was sick, but I felt calm and completely at ease with myself. Nothing needed to be different. Life was good. Of course the state of my physical body then was obviously anything but good – but even so, everything was good.

◆

*Do the Tibetans go away somewhere
to 'become spiritual'?*

◆

The point I am making is: you don't need anything or anyone in order to be spiritual. Wherever you are, no matter what the circumstances, you are always 'home' if you are connected to your true nature. What do you do when you do not feel that connection with your true nature – what we call your higher self or your 'Buddha nature'? You find it by surrendering to your life in the here and now and accepting the person you are in this very moment. There is no need for you to be anyone else but yourself. If there were, you would be someone else, right? Your body doesn't need to be better than it is right now; if it did, it would be better. You don't need to be anywhere else other than right where you are now, or you would be there. You are here, so your inner peace is here too – don't you feel it? If not, then you must learn to look deeper.

Spirituality, then, is nothing more than giving up your resistance to what is. Living spiritually is daring to see what is in front of you and daring to experience your life as it is right now. And experience means conquering our greatest human fear: living as a complete human being.

Are Emotions Anti-Spiritual?

Here's another popular misconception: spiritual life means that you avoid fights or arguments and that you can't show emotions. That you must not set boundaries. That you may not say, 'Hey, I don't have a problem with you personally, but I don't like what you're doing.' It's human to argue, to show emotions, to object to something you don't like. But in certain circles, being 'human' is seen as 'unenlightened'.

Never one to shy away from confrontation, I find that sometimes there is nothing more cleansing and clarifying then a good old-fashioned fight. Sadly, many women are under the impression that life somehow improves when you avoid disagreements and that a state of harmony can be achieved only without a struggle. Or as best-selling author Harriet Rubin says in her book *The Princessa: Machiavelli for Women*, 'Most women believe that the way to make life better is to remove bad things from it.' Personally, I would like to add that it's not just women: most people who 'busy' themselves with spirituality do this as well. I once had an experience of this kind with a girlfriend who considered herself spiritual. When I spoke out and voiced my indignation about the way she had treated a mutual friend, I apparently took the wrong tone and used the wrong words. Being direct and to the point does not seem to work for most people in these 'spiritual' circles. There they prefer to solve all problems with light, love, and nodding your head yes and saying 'I am OK with it', whatever 'it' is.

◆

You don't become a human being by floating on a cloud, but by being securely rooted to the earth.

◆

Thinking that you cannot be a spiritual being and a warrior at the same time is a huge misconception. It makes you weak. Truly spiritual people can clearly see that fighting is the ally of loving, confrontation the ally of peace and courage the ally of vulnerability. Above all, they can see that being human is the absolute prerequisite for true spirituality. 'We are a body, we are not angels,' says Dutch pastor and professor of business spirituality Paul de Blot. 'My mission is humanity. Escaping into spirituality, floating on a cloud, that's easy, it takes no discipline. But for good relationships you need a lot of damn discipline. … Without discipline you will never have human spirituality.'

I find great relief in what he says. We are not on this earth to become spiritual; we are spiritual beings whose task it is to become complete human beings. You don't become a human being by floating on a cloud, but by being securely rooted to the earth, both feet on the ground. Not by denying or suppressing your emotions, but by letting them be. By taking on the fight when love, truth and integrity ask it of you. Too often I come across people in these meaningless spiritual circles, people with a vacant look in their eyes and dead, expressionless faces, stemming from all their suppressed emotions, their stifled desires and their egos reduced to nothing. They call it being 'conscious' and 'free from attachment'. Yet to me it seems more like being completely detached from your earthly existence and not knowing how to deal with your own humanity.

◆

*Spirituality is about getting to know ourselves
by looking honestly at our lives.*

◆

Questions for a Curious Soul

- What does the concept of spirituality mean to you?

- How do you express your spiritual nature in everyday life?

- What does it mean to you to live life consciously?

- How often do you ignore the fact that you are not living according to your own inner truth, even while you are painfully aware you are going against it?

- How does it feel to deny that truth?

- What makes it so difficult to actually live by your own personal spiritual beliefs and convictions?

Half a Saint or a Whole Human?

A spiritual lifestyle has nothing to do with escaping reality and floating on the aforementioned cloud. Real, pure spirituality is solidly rooted in our own humanity. There is no 'magic' enlightenment outside of our daily lives. Spirituality is nothing more or less than being a complete, well-rounded human being, in real life, every day, again and again. What does that mean in practice? Being kinder, more loving, more trustworthy, humbler and wiser – something we can only achieve by trial and error. Learning to live according to higher laws, by which we learn how to serve the universe (or God, or nature, or life) as 'parishioners without a church' without withdrawing in silence from our lives. It is about getting to know ourselves by looking honestly at our lives. Not on a mountaintop in Tibet. No, right *here*. In the middle of the hectic West. In a life with a relationship, children, a dog, a house and bills that need to get paid.

This is not a book that promises you a life without problems and a shortcut to enlightenment. This is a book about the magic already present in your humanity and your earthly existence. I want to show you that fulfilment in your life is a lot closer than you may think. That spirituality is never something you need to seek far outside of yourself. That a spiritual life and personal growth are not as complicated as they may seem. Spiritual living doesn't mean making huge changes in your life, but changing your outlook on things and creating more space for your experience. You develop a spiritual backbone by courageously conquering your fears and, without fear, continuing on your inner journey.

◆

Real spirituality is rooted in blood and bones,
heart and spirit.

◆

This isn't a book about how you can become an exemplary human being in ten simple steps. Spiritual living has nothing to do with doing everything 'right' or being perfect. It is not about accomplishing anything in particular, improving in any way or trying to be a saint. Spiritual living at its core is living consciously. This means connecting to the highest form of truth within yourself and incorporating this into your everyday life – staying absolutely true to your higher self by listening to your heart and following the path of your soul, regardless of how difficult this may be for others to understand. Willingness to do your own inner homework is an absolute condition.

Spirituality, in other words, is your True Self. It's getting to know yourself, making contact with the part of you that will forever stay the same and letting yourself be led by it. It is surrendering to this self, letting go of ideas about how you 'should' be and how your life 'should' have been and learning to love the reality right in front of you. Real spirituality is rooted in blood and bones, heart and spirit. This spirituality is forever – everything else is an illusion.

Not Preaching but Sharing

In saying this, I am in no way trying to teach you a lesson. Rather, I'm inviting you to think, to doubt, to feel and to experience for yourself. I am not trying to preach at you, but to share my ideas, insights and experiences. I don't want you to start to think like me or do what I do. It is not my intention to seduce or compel you to travel the same road as I have. My road is not important to you.

Not long ago I gave a reading from my book *The Deeper Secret*. After the reading, I was making my way towards the exit when two women in their 30s came running up behind me. 'Annemarie, can we ask you some questions? We want to be just like you!' I was so surprised, all I could answer was, 'Believe me when I say you don't want that. *Really* you don't!' They roared with laughter.

◆

There is only one road that matters – your road.

◆

Of course it is appealing now and then to think: *If only I had that person's life, then surely I would have a very exciting existence and be very happy.* But we cannot walk each other's paths or live each other's lives. We can only do what is meant for us to do. Every individual's road to travel is paved with lessons precisely calibrated for his or her own soul. Those lessons only have one purpose: to stimulate our inner growth. They are a very personal and intimate deal between you and the Creator of the Universe (God, nature, life, or however you choose to envision it). We cannot swap experiences or lessons just because someone else's life, coming forth out of those experiences, may at first glance seem more attractive. Those girls couldn't have truly meant what they said. Because if they really became just like me, they would spend the rest of their lives sitting in a wheelchair. I suppose that thought hadn't crossed their minds.

There is only one real road that matters. That is *your* road and the opportunities you may come across on it to become the person you are capable of becoming. Everyone's life is a series of experiences and, therefore, lessons – often difficult and painful lessons. Some lessons we learn quickly, other we need to repeat a few times, because we didn't quite understand them the first time or because we are just hard-headed souls. Some lessons aren't so hard to take, but other lessons we fight tooth and nail. The important thing here is that we all hit bumps and dips in the road. These bumps are unique opportunities that ask us to become stronger, more accepting, more loving, more open and more real.

No Right or Wrong

Learning about the spiritual life is not a matter of words that you should suddenly start to believe. I have been writing spiritual books since 1995, and along the way I have learned that spiritual growth cannot be transferred simply by writing about it or talking about it. Words without the experience are empty at best. Words, at most, can inspire you to point the lens through which you see the world in a different direction.

It is experience that gives the words their power, and the experience is yours alone. There are no rules to follow. There is no right or wrong. You don't owe anyone an explanation for the life that you choose. You can live in whatever way you think is good. You're allowed to hear, taste, feel, think, until you keel over. There is no payback, because you cannot do anything wrong. You are a spiritual being that has come here to have its own unique experience – the experience of being human in a human body and everything that comes with it: feelings, emotions, thoughts, senses and, oh yeah, an ego, as your perfect earthly toolbox.

Everything is already here – everything you need to experience true happiness, love and success in your life. What we take away from each passing moment depends on how much attention we give it. How deeply we experience life reflects the depth of our own consciousness. So you have everything at hand to make this an amazing experience. Don't put your life on hold. Let it happen. Let it flow. Let life come as it will. Welcome it with all its instability and imperfection. You are not here to direct and judge. You are here to experience. So do! Stop criticizing reality, just let it go and see what happens. Open your heart and experience. That's all.

Summary

- We are not on this earth to become spiritual; we are spiritual beings that chose this earthly experience to become complete human beings.

- We don't become fully human by floating on some mystical cloud, but by being firmly rooted in the earth; not by suppressing or denying our emotions, but by letting them be.

- True spirituality has nothing to do with making changes in your life. It has to do with changing your view of things and creating room for your experience, whatever that may be. It is not about achieving anything, improving on anything or trying to be a saint. Spiritual life at its core means nothing more than living consciously and in compliance with the highest degree of truth within yourself.

- We need to learn to live according to higher laws that let us serve the universe (God, nature, life) as 'parishioners without a church' without withdrawing in complete silence from our daily lives. It's about getting to know ourselves by looking at our lives in the clearest and most honest way possible.

- There is no right and wrong. There is no payback, because you cannot do anything wrong. You are a spiritual being that has come here to have its own unique experience: namely, being a human being in a human body, with all that comes with it – feelings, emotions, thoughts, senses and ego as the very tools you need.

Chapter 2

SPIRITUALITY IS AN EXPANDED VIEW OF REALITY

How you think is what you see.
Or is what you see how you think?

— TULKU LAMA LOBSANG

*I*t is a law of life on earth that what is most obvious and logical is usually the first thing we dispute or dismiss. Case in point: we doubt what we can't see or touch. Whatever is not visible and tangible is by definition questionable, and we need to have it proven over and over again. It would seem much more logical to think that the reality we can perceive today is only a tiny part of a much larger reality, a reality that we cannot (yet) see, than to take what we can perceive now for the only reality there is. Yet still people dismiss this idea as strange or altogether wrong.

No one ever looks at the teacup on his or her desk and asks: *How can I know with absolute certainty that this teacup is real?* Because our eyes can see it, we say it exists. But could it be we're missing something? Is this cup part of something else? Do I see a cup only because I don't have the senses to see the whole reality that's present? To put it another way, do we create the material world as we know it in our minds? Are tangible things really as 'material' as they seem? Or are they just something we've thought up?

Is reality as real as it seems?

•

How can I know with absolute certainty
that this teacup is real?

•

As a child, I was already pondering these types of things. From a very young age I had an interest in philosophy, theosophy and all things invisible. I could lie on my back for hours just staring at the stars. The longer I stared, the smaller and more humble I felt, yet at the same time I had a sense of being incredibly connected. It seemed completely illogical to me, even arrogant, to think we were the only living creatures in the cosmos, and I was very curious about our 'fellow travellers'. I found it a perfectly normal idea that what we could see and touch was probably just a fragment of a bigger reality. Not that when I was ten I could put it in those grown-up words. To me it was just how it *was*. We as human beings were part of something far bigger, the sheer size, whole range and full power of which we could never wrap our minds around. The reality we were trying to see through with our minds was just a fragment of the whole.

A Unique Adventure on Planet Earth

Young as I was, the invisible reality had already become a very important part of my reality. How could it not be? When I was only 11, something completely invisible, immeasurable and thus unprovable turned my life upside down. Out of the blue, in one night, I became paralysed. I had what is called transverse myelitis. To this very day, the true cause has never been found, only guessed at. Physically, no medical cause could be definitively identified; the doctors suspected that a tick bite detected too late might have been the cause, but it was never proven. So life was challenging me to come up with my own answers to the 'why' questions – big questions in such a young human life – and all the answers I was seeking had to be found in the non-visible reality.

In the years that followed, it became increasingly clear that I had chosen my life's path before my birth. I had signed up for a unique adventure on a planet that as far as we know – as far as its features go – is not to be outdone by any other. I had come to this planet with only one goal: to experience what it was like to have this exact appearance, this exact body, these exact circumstances, and to go about living this life in my own unique way, staying true to my soul.

•

Does the universe make big mistakes, then say, 'Oops, sorry, now you'll live the rest of your life in a wheelchair'?

•

My handicap helps me to experience intensely *who I am*, and it gives me the strength to do the things I am here to do. It helps me not to overcommit or waste time doing things I am not meant to do. Does that sound crazy? To many people it probably does. They will say, 'Sure, anyone can come up with an explanation for their situation that makes their life bearable.' But for me that is really not the case. From the beginning, nothing needed to be 'made bearable' for me. I knew and felt from the start: *This is good.* I had no need to deny, repress, resist or try to fix anything. I didn't want to hear anything about how I could get 'better' anymore. I didn't feel sick, afflicted, incomplete or limited in my potential. I did, however, want to understand my situation – not just with my intellect, but with real understanding and true knowing (the kind of knowing that often comes into play only when we find ourselves in one of the freefall phases of our lives). I wanted to become conscious – to see exactly how my situation was designed for my inner growth and to understand my own personal role in the bigger plan.

Oops, Sorry!

Not surprisingly, on the subject of my personal view of life, I have come across a lot of sceptics and encountered a great deal of cynicism over the past 25 years. To be honest, though, often it really *does* surprise me. Especially when I was younger, I never understood why people couldn't put my circumstances (or their own) into a bigger picture and see them as a part of a universal plan in which we all still had our individual say. I found it strange, for instance, to view a handicap as something apart, standing on its own, a departure from the way things are supposed to be. As if it's something that life is doing to you, just like that, to annoy you. Or worse: as if the universe is capable of making really big mistakes here and there. As if to say: 'Oops, sorry! That wasn't our intention, but too bad, now you will live the rest of your life in this little wheelchair.'

I never really think in terms of 'what a pity'. I'm convinced that we aren't doing ourselves or creation any favours by looking at things in that way. I don't believe in mistakes on the part of God, nature, the universe or some big captain in the sky. Because then the whole universe would be a complete mess. It would mean that the sun and the moon just happened, by pure coincidence, to pop up in the sky in the right place every day.

Questions for a Curious Soul

- What image of yourself do you base your life on? What's your view of reality?

- Do you really believe the opportunities you see in front of you are the only opportunities there are?

- Do you believe that there may be another reality there, beyond the reality you currently experience as real?

- Do you understand that possibility is what you believe to be possible?

- Do you know that the outside world and your inner world are not two separate worlds at all, but that your outside world is shaped largely by what your inner world perceives it to be?

- If you are creating your life according to what you believe you are worth and what you think is possible for you, how could you change your reality, starting today?

Are We Our Brains?

The idea that the visible reality we 'see' is only a small part of a much larger reality has always been an obvious and natural part of life to me. Just because we can't see something with the naked eye doesn't mean we can dismiss it and say it doesn't exist. If we do, we're making the same mistake scientists have made for ages. They could not see bacteria, so to them, bacteria did not exist. How long did it take science to accept that you could become physically sick from psychological disorders? That stress could cause stomach ulcers or high blood pressure? Not long ago we were defenceless against an 'invisible' illness like tuberculosis.

•

'Ms Postma, souls don't exist!'

•

As a columnist for a daily newspaper, I have been writing on these subjects quite a bit since the late '90s. Every once in a while this has brought some angry responses my way. One reader wrote: 'Ms Postma, souls don't exist and there is no life after death. Prove to me that these fictional stories are based on truth. You can't; we are nothing more than a functioning brain!'

Imagine – believing this to be the only rationale for how the human body works? Thinking that our body is only a machine being driven by the brain? That the heart is a sort of water pump to keep things moving along? Descartes himself would have had a great big belly laugh about this. We are living in a time that asks far more of us than to see the world from such a purely mechanical perspective. This way of thinking is way past its expiration date.

Even science, if it seeks to find solutions for the problems we face today, will have to start taking a whole new approach, one that includes the 'invisible' and 'spiritual' factors. 'In the 21st century, science will be spiritual, or … there will be no science,' I read in an article by the Indian psychiatrist Dr Vikram Prabhu. 'Modern-day medical science, including psychology, has all but completely ignored the spiritual aspects of health care. Studies in the past 15 years have confirmed that spirituality plays a very big role in people's lives. It has been documented … that a firm belief in God can play a very positive part in the human healing process. … There is a very real and positive connection between prayer/spirituality and health.' In the same article Dr Prabhu quoted a colleague, the late Dr David B Larson, founder of the National Institute for Healthcare Research in Rockville, Maryland, who said: 'The mental battle people fight with their illness is put in perspective when the spiritual aspects of their life are included. There is evidence that there is a very positive influence on the process of accepting their illness.'

I once interviewed Dr Iteke Weeda, who successfully introduced the academic world in the Netherlands to spirituality with her 1996 book *Spiritualiteit en wetenschap* (Spirituality and Science). Thanks to her, spirituality became a field of study at the university level. The many collaborators who worked with her on the book – experienced in both fields – turned out to be anything but a small, exclusive group within the big world of 'science'. In fact, just the opposite.

'Science is knowledge obtained by measuring, verifying and repeating,' Dr Weeda explained. 'Only when you can physically grab and touch it is it science. This is why psychology and sociology often are not considered science, being too "soft" and not tangible enough. In the '70s a fascinating study was published on near-death experiences. There were scientists who greatly admired the extreme efficiency with which this study was conducted. The general consensus, though, was that since the researchers had never had near-death experiences themselves, how in the world could they research and document the event properly? But people who do research on schizophrenia have not been schizophrenic themselves, have they? Is that type of research done in a different way, then?'

•

Real knowledge is loving with a heart
that's unafraid to see.

•

The point is that a study is labelled unscientific because its outcome suggests that there is more between heaven and earth than the naked eye can see. That thought alone threatens to throw you off balance, make you doubt, encourage thought and foster humility. Most of all, it calls on your own sense of responsibility. 'Real knowledge is loving with a heart that's unafraid to see,' I read recently. But for this, your heart needs to be open first. It is much easier to explain away all that our minds cannot explain by relegating it to the realm of the 'unknown', the 'highly unlikely', the world of UFOs and green men from Mars.

Spirituality Isn't Unreliable or Irrational

Reality is made up of many more dimensions then the fragmentary things we can see, touch and measure. But it's not as if you can't be a clear-headed or 'rational' person once you become open to things that take place outside the bounds of our tangible world. It doesn't mean you are someone less credible or some weirdo who has parted company with his or her intellect. Rather, it means that as a curious soul you are open to what could be as well as what is. 'I believe that our soul prefers questions over answers,' writes psychotherapist Herman Cools in his book *Het schitterende duister* (The Brilliant Darkness). 'It wants to explore and experience, because it is searching for a *felt kind of knowledge* and does not gain understanding through definitions or dogmas. … Above all it asks for, as 15th-century mystic Nicholas of Cusa already knew, "learned ignorance". The courage to step into the deep abyss of the unknown.'

◆

*The invisible truth is far greater
than the one we can see and touch.*

◆

Blind faith is not to be confused with blindly follow-ing. Often it's assumed that the people who write off the unknown and the invisible as nonsense are the ones who operate most on objectivity and reason. I beg to differ. No, they operate on reason *as they see it*. That is something very different. That is a definition of reason that actually excludes everything that could raise any challenge to reason – a very limited definition of reason at best. Life is so full of secrets, there is so much we do not know, that it would be unbelievably arrogant to assume that we could understand everything simply with the use of reason. Life itself started somewhere, somehow, in a way of which we have no real understanding. The invisible truth is far greater then the one we can see and touch. It is therefore more 'unreliable' to close yourself off to an experience than to be open to the full reality.

For ages humanity denied a large part of reality, left it right out of the picture. In doing so, it separated itself from the true strength and primal knowledge all of us possess. This has to do with our human development. First there was the all-knowing church that told us how to live our lives. Later, it was science that was considered holy. Now we have landed in a time when many people want to reconnect with and restore their own inner knowledge – that primal knowledge that we possess within, but have lost sight of in the material and mechanical view of things so prevalent today, the perspective with which we think to 'solve' everything.

Seeing with Harry Potter's Eyes

Many of us, hungering for this inner knowledge, are pre-occupied with big life questions. We are ready for a broader and deeper insight into ourselves and our lives. *Who am I? Why do I exist? What am I here for? What is my place in this world and my part in the bigger picture? Where did I come from and where am I going?* Because of this, there is a growing interest in the subject of spirituality, an interest that, these days, is no longer on the fringe. Take the huge success of *The Secret*, or the movie *What the Bleep Do We Know?*, or the unprecedented success of movies like the Harry Potter series, or even the worldwide interest in my own book *The Deeper Secret*.

The fact that millions of children and adults engage with all their hearts and souls in the adventures of Harry Potter, much like the wonderful world of Tolkien, shows that these types of stories fulfil a desire for a long-lost other dimension. They appeal to the need in all of us to reconnect to the true magic of life and our entire enchanted existence. Harry Potter reminds us of a broader way of thinking, a way of life that we know, somewhere deep inside of us, to be possible. It's not only children who are searching for that missing piece. Consciously or subconsciously, we all know there is another dimension beyond the tangible material world we see. We know that we are so much more than we think.

•

How can you see something new if you only dare to see what you already know?

•

Is the Earth Flat or Round?

No change can take place outside of us unless a change takes place within. *All* change happens from the inside; after that, the outside circumstances automatically follow suit. If you honestly want to start living a more spiritual life, it is essential that you start to rethink your ideas about reality. How can you experience something new if you only dare to only see what you already know? You cannot build a new life with the same old thoughts and convictions you have always had. Think and believe the same as you did before and you will get the same result. If you keep seeing reality as a square, but strive to see life as a full circle, you have a problem. You need a 'paradigm shift'.

What is a paradigm? A paradigm is a collection of structured thought patterns, concepts, beliefs and convictions. In other words, the 'rules' that you, often subconsciously, have thought up: this should go this way, that should be that way, this is how it *is*. These rules do three things:

1. They determine your boundaries.

2. They determine how you should act within those boundaries in order to be happy, safe or successful.

3. They determine how and what your reality is.

A paradigm shift, then, means a shift to another collection of thought patterns, beliefs and convictions – a new set of 'rules'. By constantly thinking that the world is exactly as you see it, you are closing off the development and expansion of your consciousness. In effect, you are locking yourself up in a 'consciousness prison' of your own making. The bars of that prison represent the blocks of your own thoughts. Do you want to experience new things? Then you will have to create new space for them. It's about changing your core convictions about life and altering your view of reality. It's about broadening your horizons within your thought patterns, creating more space there and thereby broadening your experience!

Paradigm for a Spiritual Life: New 'Rules' for a New Game

- There is no outside world separate from your inner world.

- You create the world you perceive.

- You see only the world you allow yourself to see.

- You inhabit the world you believe in and deem possible.

- You can't experience anything new if you only allow yourself to see what you already know.

- You need to look at reality differently in order to see something different.

- There is no such thing as the real world and the unreal world. Who can say that the dream you had last night was less real than the teacup on my desk?

- You are part of something much bigger than you – part of an actual plan.

- Everything and everyone is connected.

- Your thoughts and actions influence the whole world.

- In the universe, there are no coincidences, and random events do not exist.

A Broader View Is Not a Luxury

The realization that reality is broader than the world we can see and touch is not only the beginning of a spiritual life for you personally, it is also an absolute necessity for our time. Society is up against tremendous challenges – in many areas it almost seems to be grinding to a halt – and the fact that no real solutions are found for the many problems facing our world suggests that our old way of thinking has hit a dead end. We cannot take meaningful action without looking at a broader reality than the one we can see and touch. In our old, limited thinking, we say, 'We have a shortage of earthly resources; we're going to run out!' From a new perspective, you could say, 'In reality there is no shortage, but as people we are *falling short* of our earthly resources.' Earth offers us more than enough on all fronts, only we always *think* we are running out and never have enough. Scarcity is not real. It is our thinking that creates the reality of scarcity.

●

Spirituality is not a hobby.
It's not the same as an hour of yoga at the gym.

●

'It's time for us to show up!' said physicist, author and healer Jude Currivan, sternly and emphatically, during a reading of her book *The 13th Step* that I attended in 2008. She said it several times, and it struck me very deeply. There really isn't anything casual about spirituality. It isn't a hobby. It is a way of life that is about taking responsibility for ourselves and the well-being of the greater whole. It can't be compared with an hour of yoga class at the local gym. It's about truly getting to know your thoughts and acknowledging your ability to change them – which will not only change your personal world, but let you contribute to the world we share.

It is not our body that determines who we are, it is our consciousness. If all of us accept our spiritual responsibility, society will be focused no longer on power and personal battles, but on working together. We won't be fighting and competing with each other in order to 'be someone'. It really is, as Jude Currivan said, high time for us to make a shift – *now*. To stop drawing lines that divide us and to focus on coming together instead. Only when we achieve that broader consciousness can problems like poverty, hunger, war, animal neglect and abuse and the wasting of earth's resources be solved. Only when the cynical, critical masses come to this understanding can paradise exist right here on earth.

Summary

- Just because we cannot see or touch something, we cannot say it doesn't exist. If we do, we're making the same mistakes scientists made when they could not see bacteria, so to them bacteria did not exist.

- The invisible reality is far greater than the reality we can see. So it's not irrational to be open to seeing the larger picture – it's unreasonable to close yourself off from experiencing it.

- For a long time we have denied much of what we know, deep down, to be real. In doing so we have separated ourselves from our true strength and split ourselves off from the primal knowledge all of us possess.

- Consciously or subconsciously, we are all aware there is another dimension beyond the tangible and visible one we perceive. We know we are more than we think we are.

- When it comes to solving the problems of the world, our old way of thinking is a dead-end street. The realization that reality is more than we can see is not only the start of a spiritual life for us personally, it is the change we need in our time.

- If you truly want to start living a spiritual life, a life lived from within, then it is essential that you rethink your ideas about reality (shift your paradigm). After all, how can you experience something new if you choose to see only what you already know? You cannot build a new life with the same old thoughts and convictions you had before.

Chapter 3

SPIRITUALITY IS
AN ABSOLUTE
NECESSITY

*The distinction between past, present and future
is only a stubbornly persistent illusion.*

— ALBERT EINSTEIN

*H*ave you seen the movie *Home*? No? Then I recommend you do, maybe even before you read this chapter. This movie is distributed free worldwide on the Internet. For example, you can find it at www.youtube.com/user/homeproject or simply type in *Home* in the search engine on YouTube. The movie is, in a way, like a spiritually oriented version of the 2006 release *Planet Earth*. It offers incredible images of the earth, set to great music, but more importantly, it gives hard facts about the way we humans are damaging nature, animal life, the environment and the planet. The makers of the movie are afraid that the current worldwide economic crisis will distract us from the far more urgent problems of Mother Earth herself. By focusing our attention only on the financial woes at hand, we are missing the fact that it isn't a separate problem – that everything is connected. There are no consequences without actions. The makers of *Home* want to broaden our horizons and show us the effect our current way of thinking and acting has on everything, including our precious earth.

Maybe you're thinking, *Ugh, do I really need to know all of that right now*? But that would seriously disappoint me. If you are reading this book – and let's get this straight right now – you are by definition not someone who looks away when they show whale hunts or the killing of baby seals on TV. You are not someone who doesn't want to know where the perfectly pre-packaged meat in the supermarket comes from. And you are not someone who shuts out the fact that every year 13 million acres of forest disappear. Lastly, you are not someone who doesn't want to see what effect our commerce has on nature, animals and the earth.

The earth came into existence five billion years ago. Did you know that humans have only been here for the past 200,000 years, but that just in the last 50 years the earth has changed dramatically as a result of our big, destructive footsteps? Did you know it took the earth four billion years to create trees, with their amazing ability to hold oxygen, which in turn allows us to exist? Where do we show our respect for this process in the way we treat the earth? In barely 40 years we have destroyed 20 per cent of the Amazon rain forest. We use the soil for growing animal feed (soya) and turn a forest into meat!

Spirituality is often seen as 'soft', while the truth is considered hard. But spirituality is nothing more than acknowledging that your personal choices have consequences. It means allowing the truth in and living honestly. A spiritual way of life is a realistic way of life – one of taking personal responsibility. Do you realize that one billion people don't have healthy water to drink, and 5,000 people a day die from contaminated water? That one billion people are suffering and hungry, while we use more than 50 per cent of the world's grain to feed cattle? That every single day 40,000 children die from malnutrition? All horrors brought to light by *Home*.

What effect do you think the mass production of all that meat has on the natural balance of the earth? Most people don't know that the production of vegetable protein takes far less energy then the production of animal protein. It takes 10 times less soil, 11 times less fossil fuel and 100 times less water! To cultivate soya for human consumption, rather than for cattle feed, is far less damaging to the rain forest, the lungs of the earth. A British study published in the journal *The Lancet* explains that eating less meat also helps in the battle against the greenhouse effect. The mass production of cattle is responsible for a quarter of our total global emission of greenhouse gases. Switching to a different feed doesn't change anything, according to the study. But if people were to eat 10 per cent less meat, the emissions would remain the same until 2050, even if the world population grew significantly.

•

A spiritual way of life is a realistic way of life.

•

Spirituality Is an Ethical Choice

There are many reasons to eat healthy and pure food. You will feel clearer-minded and more energetic, remain at your natural weight and look better overall. But beyond that there is the ethical side of things, which is often ignored. Choosing to eat truly healthy food, though, is ethical by definition. When you buy and eat healthy food, you check where it comes from and you understand how your eating habits affect the rest of the world, the greater whole.

On top of that, everything on your plate is energy. Pure food is loaded with energy that is also pure. Personally, I would prefer to not have something on my plate that comes from an industry that should be hiding its head in shame because it's such a painful example of our blatant disrespect for nature, animals and, therefore, ourselves.

◆

There is no excuse for looking away from suffering,
no matter what life forms it concerns.

◆

I have been a vegetarian since I was 11 years old. I simply didn't like the taste of meat. Since my mother cooked macrobiotic, I wasn't used to eating meat anyway. The older I got, the more I started educating myself about nutrition and health, and I found that my vegetarianism became more and more a spiritual and ethical ideal. If we didn't need to kill animals to stay healthy, then why would we? As humans we have so many alternatives. The idea that eating meat is a sign of wealth and prosperity is a thing of the past; now it only contributes to the extreme poverty on our earth.

Even as a child, I had a hard time grasping why humans were so reckless with animal rights and why we so readily claimed it as our right to decide their fate. As an adult, I still don't know why. Respecting the earth means respecting ourselves. Fighting for the rights of animals is also fighting for ourselves. Philosopher Peter Singer, author of the book *The Way We Eat: Why Our Food Choices Matter*, says respect for animals is mainly a moral choice. It is. It's the same as being deeply affected by suffering. There is no excuse for looking away from suffering, no matter what life form it concerns. There should be no difference. Animals are not 'products', but living creatures that can experience joy and pain and, just like you and me, have a right to safety and quality of life. This means we have to stop being constant invaders into their lives.

Mea Culpa!

So, vegetarianism is my own personal protest against our neglect and betrayal of animals and of nature herself. For me, boycotting meat (as well as other products from the farm industry, such as battery chicken eggs) is a form of protest. Without taking such a stand, I believe, we will just go on exhausting and depleting our earth, as well as perpetuating many forms of animal abuse.

◆

*I believe in putting energy in motion,
in righteous indignation and the power of love.*

◆

It's easy to stand on the sidelines shouting 'No way!' to protest animal abuse that happens in faraway places. Like bullfighting in Spain, the eating of dog meat in Korea or the clubbing of baby seals in Canada. It is far more difficult to reconcile your love and respect for animals, or your concern for the troubles of the earth, with your actions closer to home. It is hard to act on your spiritual ideals in real, everyday life.

It's not as if I am always perfectly consistent. I try my best, but I certainly – and knowingly – cross the line here and there. I wear leather jackets. I'm not exactly keeping the promise I made to myself and Mother Earth to consume less. I take milk in my coffee, though I really despise everything the dairy industry stands for. I often leave the water running too long while brushing my teeth, and I don't always read the labels in my T-shirts to make sure they didn't come from some hideous child-labour factory. Mea culpa! However, that doesn't mean I get carried away with all my imperfections and decide that nothing I do or don't do makes a difference.

Deep down, we know what we need to do and not do, and when we go against our conscience, we start to feel more and more uneasy. Our body, for example, may give us signals that it no longer enjoys eating large amounts of meat. Those who in this day and age are still careless and rude enough to toss an empty soda can on the ground will surely look over their shoulders to check if anyone saw them do it. Boundaries shift. The reasoning we used to rationalize and trivialize certain destructive behaviour in the past no longer holds up. But that doesn't mean that everyone will *do* better just because we know better.

Don't misunderstand me – I am not trying to justify any behaviour. But I also don't want it to seem as if living a true spiritual life – even for me – doesn't cost a bit more effort than the alternative on some days. However, I am no fatalist. I absolutely believe in the positive power of the individual. I believe in putting energy in motion, in the power of righteous indignation and the power of love. As humans, we are capable of so much love, but we reserve it only for our loved ones. We are capable of so much creativity, but we don't use it enough. We go in circles like hamsters on a wheel. Isn't it hard to fathom that we have the ability to solve so many problems, but simply *choose* not to?

Questions for a Curious Soul

- Do you see reality as a collection of separate things or creatures, or do you feel connected to everything and everyone alive?

- Do you believe that the earth has a physical body, a soul and consciousness, just as we humans do? That we, humans as well as animals, are part of a highly sensitive, energetic, cosmic system?

- Do you think the history books will one day describe us as people who weren't bad, just very confused, because we had no idea of the larger connection we share and because we didn't understand that humans' abusive behaviour towards each other, animal life and nature would come right back at us like a big moral boomerang?

- How do you contribute, with your way of thinking and living, to raising our consciousness in unity and love?

- Do you know that you can do so right now by the way you follow your conscience and carry yourself in life?

- Do you understand that by your actions and the daily choices you make, you have a huge positive impact on the greater whole?

Spirituality Means Finding Another Way

We live in one giant force field. This means that humans and nature influence each other endlessly. That every action you or I take has an effect on the rest of the world. A dysfunctional way of thinking and acting has a ripple effect on everything – literally. Nothing stands alone, nothing is separate. Everything is energy, so a disturbance in the energy field over here causes a corresponding disturbance over there. Even the smallest decision isn't exempt from the continuous process of cause and effect (what we might also call karma). This law applies to everyone, always. It is also known as the butterfly effect. According to this theory, a small action can have huge consequences. So when a butterfly flaps its wings in Brazil, it might cause a typhoon somewhere in Asia.

◆

A spiritual life means seeing into the core of things.

◆

In other words, humanity has a far greater effect on everything than we realize. If we knew our own strength, we would certainly realize that we could change the world simply by starting with ourselves. But of course nothing will change for those who close their eyes to what is. A real spiritual life means seeing into the core of things. You realize some truths may be hard, but only those truths you still need to crack open.

In the movie *Home*, we're told, 'It is too late to be pessimistic.' Maybe we should change this to 'It is too late not to be spiritual.' Our spiritual development isn't about our individual well-being anymore, but about the health and well-being of nature, animals and the earth. As long as we don't see that our fate is inevitably tied to all that, we will keep making the kinds of choices that have brought us to where we are today. 'We all know this, but refuse to believe it,' says the voice in the movie. We know we are depleting our earth, but yet we don't acknowledge it.

So is there a solution to this enormous mess we continue to make? Sure! Just *accept* it. Because people only change when they run out of options – that's who we are. So, by all means, let's keep ploughing along in our perpetual state of stupidity, fishing our oceans dry, pumping every last bit of oil and gas out of the earth. Let's mow down all the trees we can, drive even more cars, eat more beef and chicken to create more strange deadly viruses, fight more wars, elect more small-minded right-wing politicians and bring even more misunderstandings into the world. Until finally the ice caps melt, the earth is flooded and poor Noah can start from scratch with his Ark.

◆

What kind of world do you want to live in?
What are you willing to do to get there?

◆

Or can we do it differently? I would like to keep believing that we can. With every opportunity we are given to do it another way, we can. We all have that opportunity – hundreds of times a day. Even as you read this now, you are being given the opportunity. We are free, each time, to make use of these moments. In the eyes of the universe, mistakes don't exist, only experiences. However, the law of cause and effect *does* exist. At any point we are free to choose – to act or not act. But we will always reap what we have sown, not as a punishment but as a consequence. Look at your life. Do you want a purer, more honest life? Then you need to be more honest with yourself and live more truthfully. You are allowed to experience everything, but nothing comes without consequences. So the question is: what do you want in the future, how do you want your life to be and what kind of world do you want to live in? What are you willing to do to get there, starting today?

Summary

- Spirituality is often seen as 'soft', while the truth seems hard. But true spirituality is nothing more than acknowledging that your personal choices have consequences, allowing the truth in and living truthfully.

- We live in one giant force field. This means that humans and nature are endlessly influenced by each other, but also that every action you or I take can affect what happens in the world. Even the smallest decision can't be made without taking the law of cause and effect into consideration. This law applies to everyone, always.

- A dysfunctional way of thinking and acting has an effect on everything around us. Nothing stands on its own; everything is energy. So disturbing the energy field here will cause a disturbance somewhere else.

- Spirituality is not a passing fad or luxury – it is an absolute necessity for our world.

- It is too late not to be spiritual. Our spiritual development is no longer about individual well-being, but about the health and well-being of nature, animal life and the earth itself.

- The question is: how do you want your life to be and what kind of world do you want to live in? What are you prepared to do in order to achieve this? Will you start right now?

- Humankind has a far greater influence on the whole than we realize. If we knew our true power, we would know that we absolutely can change the world, starting with ourselves. But nothing can ever change for those who close their eyes to what is.

Chapter 4

SPIRITUALITY IS
TAKING RESPONSIBILTY

*Every cause that has not yet produced its effect
is an event that has not yet come to completion.*

— GARY ZUKAV

I once saw a TV 'reality' show in which two young professional women were getting help in their battle to lose weight. They were both too heavy and out of shape to pass the fitness test that would admit them to the school of their dreams. The television dietician offered her support. Tears of gratitude poured down the young women's faces. Even their husbands chimed in to say how much they thought the ladies deserved to realize their dream.

They had seven weeks to lose the extra pounds and to improve their stamina. But things went all wrong in week four, when they went on vacation to Thailand and gained pounds instead of losing them. 'How can this be?' asked the dietician angrily upon their return. 'In Thailand the food is so light and healthy!' The girls acted surprised and even offended. All they had seen in Thailand was fish and chips! Besides, weren't they allowed to enjoy their well-deserved holiday? And another thing – they thought the dietician was being very harsh! Couldn't she show a little more sympathy? The camera zoomed in on their crying faces. When they took the test, of course, they both failed.

◆

*You can't make bad choices
and bargain your way out of the results.*

◆

I saw in this a clear and amusing example of how we always want to take the easy way out and how aggravated people get when they are confronted with their own responsibility. If these young women had done absolutely everything they could to lose the weight in order to achieve their big dream, then their tears of disappointment would have been very real. But these were tears of useless negotiating with the universe. You cannot make destructive, negative choices and expect a constructive, positive outcome. You are denying the law of karma if you believe that you can make bad choices and bargain your way out of the results. This is the very definition of wanting impossible things, and it is at the core of all the pain and sadness in our lives.

Our possibilities are endless, and if we operate with integrity (meaning we act on what we know to be true and do not break promises to ourselves), then the whole universe will converge to help us. But if we say we want one thing but do something else and still expect to get what we want … then what? That's like pushing the button on the vending machine for a can of Coke because it's cheaper, when you really want the more expensive Fanta, and then being disappointed when the can of Coke comes out.

The law of cause and effect is not a simple point system that's racking up punishments and keeping score. The universe does not judge. The law of karma is our own impersonal, universal, non-judgemental teacher of responsibility. It is the most important law of nature, and it justifies everything in life. Are you someone who is constantly and ruthlessly judging the mistakes of others? Then without a doubt you will one day make a huge, painful mistake and get very little understanding from the people around you. You get what you give. You will not receive what you cannot give. You can act in ignorance, but then at some point you will be confronted with your own ignorance. You can cheat on your partner, but one day someone will cheat on you. You can eat meat every day, but the rain forest in Brazil will pay the price. You can go through life reckless and heartless, but one day the chaos will catch up with you. You can make destructive choices, but from those choices you cannot expect a constructive outcome. This is the unrelenting logic of karma, with which you cannot negotiate.

◆

The law of cause and effect is not about keeping score.

◆

Karma and its corollary, reincarnation, are not just Eastern concepts; you can also find them in the works of the philosopher Plato, in the teachings of Judaism and even in early Christianity. Up until the fifth century, reincarnation was being taught by the highest Christian authorities. But after this time, the teachings went underground and were mainly taught in secret. In the same way, reincarnation and karma are not spooky occult ideas. They both point to our character and circumstances in this life being determined by the thoughts, deeds and desires of a *past* life. And this means simply that we are responsible for our own lives. Nothing and no one else – not even a power outside of us – can undo the effects of our deeds. Everyone today is the sum total of all his or her lives combined. Each and every one of us develops spiritually through the conscious effort we put forth during our sequence of lifetimes.

'If No Harm Is Done, So It Shall Be'

At an exhibition of work by my friend Margje Teeuwen, an artist, two of her pieces caught my attention. I bought them on the spot. It was only later that I noticed the Wiccan text written into the paintings: *If no harm is done, so it shall be.* It would be great if everyone had this text taped to the refrigerator or hanging above his or her desk.

◆

You cannot negotiate with karma.

◆

A good choice for you can truly be a good choice only if it causes no harm to others or to life. If you give up even a small part of your integrity – in other words, if you are doing something that you know deep inside will have a negative effect for you, someone else or anything else, no matter how trivial it seems – then you are creating a negative cause-and-effect relationship. Spiritual living, therefore, is simply being conscious and trying to live according to the highest truth of this very moment. We only know what we know now. But every time you know better and don't act better, you are damaging your integrity, your own wholeness; you are chipping away a small piece of yourself.

We don't create karma when we really do not know better; we create karma when we know better but don't *do* better. When we know the truth but do not live truthfully. Luckily, karma is just as powerful when it comes to positive deeds and intentions. You experience this law in whatever way you live your life. The most important thing to remember about karma is that it is about what you are doing *right now*. You live *right now*, so everything that comes your way now is a new invitation to act with integrity and purity and thereby create new karma. Every moment is a great opportunity to get rid of your old, negative, self-destructive thought patterns. Do so not only with your deeds, but also with your thoughts, feelings and convictions. Those create karma too.

◆

We don't create karma when we really don't know better; we create karma when we know better but don't do better.

◆

The Goal of the Soul

Yes, you may say, but what does it mean when something really bad happens? What if, for example, you have a child with cancer or a disability? That is a totally understandable question, but it shows that you have not fully shifted your paradigm to true spiritual living. Either you understand how the principle of cause and effect (karma) works – or you don't. You integrate into your life the principle that you are part of a bigger whole – or you don't. You believe that there is no coincidence or randomness in the universe – or you don't. You cannot say, 'I believe in karma, but now that my daughter has ended up in a wheelchair I find life unfair.' That is just not how a spiritual life works. You don't strive to live by spiritual values only when it's convenient for you. They are being tested, and their true meaning is making itself known, precisely when you are being asked to accept the thing that seems unacceptable, to keep an open heart in the moment when you would rather retreat into bitterness, and to have faith when there is nothing safe or familiar to hold on to.

The circumstances you are in at this very moment were chosen by your soul in order to have the best chance to grow and to teach others something as well. Most people can look at some things with 'spiritual eyes' and therefore let them go easily. Everything we don't set much store by, we can turn over to the universe and see as part of the bigger plan (or the work of God). When things happen that ask us to stretch ourselves to our limits, things that force us out from behind the walls of our familiar thoughts, feelings and beliefs, we suddenly feel we're being asked to take too big a step. But taking this step, as we've seen, forces us to create more space for reality. It invites us to give new ideas, new concepts about how life works, a chance. For this you have to let go of thinking 'in bounds'. But this stretch, this shift, is new to a lot of people, and it often leaves them without the support they're used to. In the really difficult moments, it's much easier to say, 'Life is hard, life is not fair,' because that way you don't have to take any responsibility. The principle of karma, and therefore spiritual living, is not something you can apply just when it's convenient. It *always* applies – yes, even when you become ill, your child becomes ill or you lose someone you love.

•

Life on earth is not about payback.

•

Author Neale Donald Walsch said of this in his first (and best) book, *Conversations with God*: 'Do not assume that a soul which has incarnated in a body which you call limited has not reached its full potential, for you do not know what that soul was *trying to do*. You do not understand its *agenda*. You are unclear as to its *intent*.

'Therefore *bless every* person and condition, and give thanks. Thus you affirm the perfection of God's creation – and show your faith in it. For nothing happens by accident in God's world, and there is no such thing as coincidence. Nor is the world buffeted by random choice, or something you call fate.

'If a snowflake is utterly perfect in its design, do you not think the same could be said about something as magnificent as your life?'

Obviously we do not know what the agenda, or goal, of the soul is when it comes to a child who becomes ill or who has a disability. That is an intimate situation between that person and the Creator, not always clear to the outside world. I don't think anyone can ever fully understand why I, as a child, had no problem with my disability, but always felt, *This is my life, this feels right.*

♦

Some people have 'seen the light'
but have no idea where the light switch is.

♦

Children are not yet trained in wanting things to be different than they are. Things just are the way they are. Without exception, I and the other seriously ill children I shared rooms with in hospitals or rehabilitation centres were never thinking about what might have been. We had made peace with our situations, much more so than our parents ever did. We were more worried about the hardship it caused our parents than sad for ourselves. Who decides what the yardstick is for good or bad luck? Who decides if someone is to be envied or pitied? No one else but we ourselves. Only we can sense deep inside what is waiting for us in this life and stay alert to recognize the lessons and directions that lie hidden in particular events or situations.

There's No Such Thing as Good or Bad Karma

I still have a feeling I should say more about karma. On another TV show I saw, amateur chefs competed with each other to win Best Amateur Chef of the Year or something like that. Their assignment was to lure a big shellfish out of its shell and kill it. One of the girls called out, 'There goes all my good karma!' to which another chef responded, 'Yeah, she thinks she's killing her dead grandmother.' There are so many misunderstandings about karma and reincarnation, and many people use the term in the broad sense of today's popular Western spirituality. ('Wow, she's got some really bad karma!') They vaguely know something about the relationship between cause and effect – you reap what you sow – but it pretty much stops there. They have 'seen the light' but have no idea where the light switch is. Some people think that it's possible to return to earth as a dog, a cat or a frog. This is not the case. Evolution is a forward-moving consciousness, progressing and evolving. Reincarnating as an animal is not possible.

•

*It is not a punishment from God or Allah
to have a disabled body in this life.*

•

I find it remarkable that even in cultures where karma and reincarnation are key tenets of the religion, often people still don't understand exactly what karma is. It is not a punishment from God or Allah if you have a disabled body, nor is there any truth to the notion that God or Allah will reward you with 7,000 virgins if you commit a terrorist act. This is simply *not* how karma works. Karma has nothing to do with good and bad; the law of karma does not judge. So there is no such thing as 'bad' karma 'or 'good' karma – there is only K A R M A. In some cultures, they would believe that I must have done terrible things in my past lives because I have a physical disability now; I must be a terrible person to have ended up in a wheelchair in this lifetime. Many disabled children in the world are outcasts thanks to this delusion, abandoned by their families and society because they are thought to be possessed or evil. When I lived in East Amsterdam during my college years, one night a Moroccan neighbour rang my doorbell. With the best of intentions, she said to me, 'I've mobilised all my sisters. If you like, all of us can give you a massage with special oils on Saturday to drive out the devil.'

You Don't 'Have' Karma – You Are Your Karma

Very early in my youth, I came to meet – by 'coincidence' – the chairman of the Theosophical Society and connected for the first time with theosophy. As a teenager, I was consumed by it and spent many weekends at the Theosophical Lodge, where I was, not surprisingly, the only one my age. With open ears and great enthusiasm I followed all the lessons about predestination, karma and reincarnation. For almost 23 years I devoured every issue of the magazine *Theosophical Perspectives* (which sadly doesn't exist in the Netherlands anymore). All the information that my soul had longed for, I found in theosophy, because

it is such a scientific, philosophical, totally non-dogmatic
view of the world. Theosophy felt like a homecoming to
me, and since my teenage years it has shaped my view
of self-development, spirituality and life. I also devoured
books by Helena Blavatsky, G de Purucker, James A Long
– but nothing, besides life itself, taught me as much about
spirituality as theosophy did. So I learned much about
karma in my youth. And beyond the intellectual study of
this knowledge, whenever I felt deep inside what it would
mean for my own life, my own disability and my whole
view of existence, I always had a sense of justice. It gave
me trust and the feeling of being completely free all at
once, while living what, in many ways, must have seemed
a very limited life. Because of this early learning, I have
always, in the most heart-wrenching situations, been able
to find the beauty and virtue in any circumstances.

There is no God outside of us who determines what
our destiny will be. Karma is not something outside of
us; we *are* our karma. We create the fate that we experience now or later. Everything that happens to us we create,

consciously or subconsciously; we made ourselves what we are today; we will make ourselves into what we become in the future. Each and every one of us leads a life, in body or spirit, that coincides with our own thoughts and deeds.

•

There is no God outside of us who determines our destiny.
We create our fate.

•

This does not mean, though, that you can say without a doubt that I am paying with my disability for a misdeed in a past life. That certainly could be the case, but it could just as easily not be.

It is very difficult, if not impossible, to explain the karma of another person. How do we know what someone else's soul needs in order to be free? Each one of us has (or, more precisely, *is*) his or her own karma and knows, when in contact with the soul and in possession of self-knowledge, what this karma means for him or her personally in this life. I do know some people who can do this for others. They are able to sense what someone's 'soul history' is. They can tell, by looking at your life today, what karmic lines were laid in the past that have resulted in the circumstances you are living out and may or may not finish in this lifetime. But such people are very rare.

Punishment or Privilege?

I am the ambassador for the Dutch Foundation for the Disabled Child. Because I grew up with a disability, and because as an adult I live with a visible disability, I speak from deep and personal experience. I know the hoops you have to jump through as a disabled youth to get from a disadvantaged place to creating your own opportunities and taking your fully fledged position in society. I know how important it is for children to learn to make peace with their disabilities and to bring out their inner power and strength. I know how important it is to give all children the feeling that they matter and that they are welcome in this world, no matter how imperfect their outside appearance seems, no matter how burdensome their bodies are.

It is so important for them to be children, to participate in life unconditionally and carefree. Children with a disability have the right, just like any other child, to grow and develop. For them, this is just as important as it is for other kids, if not more so. They are already trapped in small, disabled bodies, so it's important to make their world as big as possible. To create a world in which they can come to life. There are still many obstacles in the road, let's not forget – many preconceived notions to overcome. We do not overcome them by seeing to it that children with a disability 'fit in' in this world, but by making sure that this world is fit for *them*. It's not about pointing out what they can't (or can no longer) do, but about encouraging them and helping strengthen their willpower, perseverance and creativity to bring out their full potential.

•

People with healthy bodies are not
higher up the spiritual ladder – only reaping
in a different way what they have sown.

•

It's on these children's behalf that I most need to clear up misunderstandings about karma. No disabled person is taking a 'punishment' by living in a damaged body. That is the utmost nonsense. Living my own life, having the connection I have with my best friend Monique, who is also in a wheelchair, and making the amazing contact I do with children who have physical or mental disabilities – all this has made it clear to me that a 'damaged' outer form is no punishment, but rather a privilege that allows you to live at a very conscious level and unapologetically make your contribution to the lives of others. It's a lot like wearing a custom-fitted suit, made to fit perfectly so you can carry out the assignment your soul chose. To become 'whole', our soul has to bring its energy into balance by fully experiencing the events. Each one of us (whether in a disabled body or mind or not) has, at one point or another on our karmic path, felt the consequences of our past thoughts or deeds. People with 'healthy' bodies are not by definition purer or higher up on the spiritual ladder. They are only reaping in a different way what they sowed in the past.

Spirituality Is What You Do Right Now

Life on earth is not about payback. Karma it all about acting right *now*, according to what you know, with the consciousness that you have right *now*. It's about what you do *now*, using your experience to find depths within you deeper than you have ever known before, in order to reach the conclusion that this has been for your good. No other experiences could move you to go that deep until now. The law of cause and effect is a strict law, but also a compassionate law. Who you are and where you are is the logical effect of who you chose to be before – in this life, or in lives before this. Cause-and-effect relationships exist in this life now, but are spread out over our various lives too. Even if you are not responsible for the causes as we see them all around us today, this doesn't exempt you from the responsibility to take them seriously and to make sure you are not a *new* cause of damaging effects on humanity, animal life and nature in the future. Karma does not make us helpless against the powers of the cosmos: it makes us part of a plan in which we can have our own say.

•

Real spirituality is not soft and fluffy – it's tough as nails.

•

Spirituality Is Not for Wimps

It is high time for us to get rid of all the *soft* and *fluffy* associations around spirituality. Real spirituality is tough as nails. It is about the ability to feel connected to all things living and the realization that we are all part of a greater whole. Spiritual living is acknowledging the unrelenting law of karma and therefore the *fundamental oneness of everything that is*. It's certainly not for wimps! It's not for people stuck in wishful thinking and magical fantasies about a world full of love and light. These will always remain beautiful fantasies if we do not take our individual responsibility and face reality with both feet on the ground. We need to understand that with our old way of thinking we will get the exact same results each time, so it is time to get rid of the old way of thinking and replace the old paradigms with new ones that give us access to the New Era. We need to cultivate a new way of thinking, new convictions, that teach us how to grow and move from *surviving* to *living*, from *having* to *being*, and from focusing on *success* to focusing on *well-being*. Or, as someone told me years ago – and I think this goes for you too – 'The universe invites you now to become someone who is making a life, rather than a living.'

Our way of thinking needs an overhaul – and we are being 'helped' by the most unlikely-seeming events to finally make the leap of consciousness that this requires. 'Is the financial crisis a curse or a blessing?' someone asked me in a TV interview. 'A blessing,' I answered. The financial crisis (just like a tsunami or an act of terrorism, for example) is not a cause, but an effect, drawn into being by the magnetic force of our thinking. It is a symptom of our spiritual separatism and the deep spiritual crisis in our world.

◆

It's time to ask a new question:
What does life want from me?

◆

So it's not a case of saving what you can while the house is on fire and then restoring everything to its former glory. We don't need to get back to the same old way we were; we need to become *new*! The solutions put forth by the old way of thinking are not solutions at all, because they come from the same source that gave us the problems. That way we're just going from bad to worse. Those who want to be part of the solution, not part of the problem, take their own responsibility, see all that happens as an invitation to a different way of thinking – thinking in terms of oneness rather than separation – and let the chaos of the world inspire them to create real change.

That's why I told the interviewer that the financial crisis was a blessing. All these things happen to force us into a different way of thinking. They invite us to truly broaden our horizons, to see reality in a new light, to stop exploiting the earth and improve life for one another and for our planet. Spirituality is insight: the insight that the luxury of thinking and acting as if we are all separate is a thing of the past; that every unkind human act towards nature and one another will come flying right back at us and crash into our heads like a boomerang.

'It's easy to make a buck. It's a lot tougher to make a difference,' said the well-known NBC television journalist Tom Brokaw, and he was right. It is time to stop thinking we can fill up the emptiness in our souls with things and money, the never-ending cycle of wanting 'more' and 'better'. It's time to stop asking ourselves what we want and need from life and start asking different questions: *What can I contribute? How can I serve life? What does life want from me?*

Summary

- The law of cause and effect is not a system of punishment. It is the most important law of nature, and it justifies everything in life.

- A good choice for you can truly be a good choice only if it brings no harm to others or to any living thing.

- If you give up any part of your integrity – in other words, if you do something that deep inside you know will have negative results for yourself or others – then you are creating a negative cause-and-effect relationship.

- Spiritual living is nothing more than being conscious and trying to live life according to the highest level of truth available to you in this very moment.

- We don't create karma when we don't know better; we create karma when we know better but don't *do* better – when we know the truth but don't live truthfully. Each time we do this, we chip away a little piece of ourselves.

- There is no God outside of us who decides our destiny. Karma is not an outside force that acts on us; we *are* our karma.

- Karma does not make us helpless before the power and strength of the cosmos. On the contrary, karma makes us part of a plan in which we each have our own input.

- Everything that happens to us we create, consciously or subconsciously; we make ourselves who we are today and what we will be in the future.

- Even if you individually are not the cause of the effects we experience in the world today, it doesn't relieve you of the responsibility to take them seriously and use that awareness to make sure you don't become a *new* cause of any negative effect in time to come.

Chapter 5

SPIRITUALITY IS
WHAT YOU DO

Spirituality is the inside of things.
Everything has a spiritual inside.
It is the depth of everything we do –
the inspiration.

— PAUL DE BLOT

*E*arly one morning while I was in my kitchen getting ready to start writing this chapter, I received my Daily Message from Neale Donald Walsch:

•

I believe God wants you to know …

Annemarie …

that all that Life asks is that you move through Life with a reverence for Life. Yet this reverence for Life must be displayed in all things. Even in the littlest things. Perhaps especially so. For instance, if you choose to consume animals, do you limit your purchases of flesh to cook to only those suppliers who treat animals humanely? Do you even know who those suppliers are? Does this matter to you? How you treat other Life Forms does matter. It says something about how you want Life to be. You see, we are creating all of this.

All of this.

•

His message carried the very quality of absoluteness that I knew I wanted to write about in this chapter. Spirituality, like love, is indivisible. You live in love – or you don't. You love someone – or you don't. It has nothing to do with circumstances. It's just like being pregnant: you either are or you aren't; you can't be a little bit pregnant. So you live spiritually – or you don't. There is no in-between, and there is no on/off switch. It's not something you do one moment and don't do the next. You are not spiritual only when it's convenient.

Spiritual living consumes your entire being, down to the smallest details. It determines the nature of your thoughts, the way you carry yourself, the choices you make and the actions you take. It also determines – as Walsch wrote – what you eat. It means that you care where your food comes from. You cannot say, 'Yeah, I live spiritually, but I still like getting my meat at the lowest possible price.' Or 'Of course I care about the earth, but I think a tropical hardwood terrace in my garden would be great.' Why not? For the simple reason that if you live spiritually, then you are conscious of your connection to all life forms. Because of that, you don't want to feed yourself with food produced in a way that caused suffering for another life form or furnish your own environment with materials whose production process contributes to destroying the earth.

◆

*Spirituality is like being pregnant . . .
and you can't be a little bit pregnant.*

◆

Seeing the world from a spiritual standpoint, there are no dividing lines between you and anyone else. We are all part of a subtle, energetic, cosmic system. There is, as I mentioned in the last chapter, no difference between nature and us, because we are part of nature. There is no 'us' and 'animals'. We are not the supreme ruling beings of this universe – even though many of us think we are. Animals aren't 'products', and they aren't just here for us; rather, we are here – precisely because of our capacity for being conscious – for *them*. It is our task to protect them and treat them respectfully. It is our duty to treat the planet – which we did not make, but where we are only guests – very delicately. There are no separate worlds; all living creatures are one. Everything is energy, so all your intentions, thoughts and actions have an energetic influence on the whole. They say something about how you want the world you live in to look. So spirituality is much more than just the realization of being connected. It is what you do with this knowledge daily, how you express what you know by the way you live your life.

Spirituality Is Self-Knowledge

Yoga, meditation, silent retreats. Spiritual techniques are being used like aspirins for the soul; we treat them as prescriptions for bliss, ecstasy or peace of mind, ways to achieve another state of being (other than where we are now) or to improve ourselves in some way. *Anything* is better than the reality of this moment. I once read a clever review by Byron Katie of *The Secret*. That book, of course, tells us how we can turn positive thoughts into tangible reality. She wrote: 'But reality is already the best thing that could be manifested. When you realize this, you're home free.' Well said.

Meditation, or any spiritual technique, is not about 'achieving' something, 'improving on' anything or making you a better person. It's about creating more space within your experience to be able to see the whole truth clearly and face it willingly – to see who and where you really are. Yes, even (or especially) when you are out of balance, or desperately seeking answers outside of yourself, or longing for stability, or feeling unworthy and abandoned by everyone else. Seeing these moments through spiritual eyes, facing them and not walking away, *that's* what it's about. These are the inner struggles that we always prefer to avoid, but that we actually need so we can awaken. By allowing them in, by going through the eye of the storm instead of skirting around it, you will receive the insights you need in order to grow spiritually. There's no need to repress or hide our fears, frustrations, neuroses and negative processes. We do much better to embrace them, learn to accept them and use them as positive material for our development. Only then can we let them go and live in complete freedom.

◆

You can burn incense until you fall over,
but it's meaningless unless you understand
what practising spirituality really means.

◆

Spirituality is about self-knowledge, self-acceptance and self-compassion. This calls for self-reflection and an inner search. Not with the goal of making us into narcissistic, monomaniacal people. Just the opposite: someone who finds inner peace is able to connect better with others and maintain far more balanced relationships. Spirituality connects people and prevents them from locking themselves up inside themselves. As you cultivate self-compassion, you can broaden your compassion for the world outside of yourself. Those who live more spiritually become hyper-aware of the reality outside themselves, and therefore – drawing on their deep connection to self – they connect to other people and to all things that are.

Spiritual living asks us to take responsibility for ourselves and to be brutally honest with ourselves. This is generally not a human being's best trait. This definitely goes for people who are obsessed with the outer appearances of spirituality. You can always seem to find them in their perfect little outfits, in all the right places with all the right people. For them, as for many people, the spiritual journey is all about ritual: meditation, reading spiritual books, taking part in certain workshops, performing certain ceremonies. This kind of practice is not based in personal responsibility or honest, searching self-reflection; it is driven by the ego, which opportunistically tries to turn spiritual values to its advantage, seeking control, support, acknowledgement and validation and trying to get a grip on life itself.

The Spiritual Puppet Show

Reading about spirituality, writing and talking about it, is one thing, but actually applying spirituality – really *doing it* – is quite another. You can go to yoga class religiously every week, attend Vipassana retreats, sign up for an intuitive art class, do your daily sun salutations, visit mediums and tarot readers, dig around in your previous lives and burn incense until you fall over. In the end, it is all empty symbolism, a puppet show, as long as you don't understand what *practising* a spiritual life truly means. That it is not about making yourself into something 'special' or fighting to prove your uniqueness.

Spirituality is not something to show off; it's not an excuse for an ego trip. But often this seems to be how it's viewed. Young supermodels go on one silent retreat in a five-star hotel in fairytale Thailand, suddenly 'see the light', come home and turn their lives upside down, trying to be little gurus themselves. They have seen someone else do something and thought, 'Hey, that looks interesting. I can *do* something with that! You know what? When I get home I'm going to "translate authentic Eastern spirituality into a Western way of life" and then give cute little yoga lessons on cute designer yoga mats!' These people don't realize that really spiritual people don't really 'look spiritual', don't travel in spiritual circles, don't refer to themselves as spiritual and certainly don't feel they have to prove how spiritual they are. For the most part they are just people who aren't afraid to be completely themselves; who carry themselves with integrity, not as better than, but certainly not as *less* than, who they are; who cultivate self-awareness and claim their authentic power. They're people who can listen to others but can also tell a good story themselves. They're people who know who they are, but are also open to the reality of others – whatever that may be.

In so-called spiritual circles you often find people who, with their carefully crafted appearance and 'spiritually correct' chit-chat, make the word *spirituality* into an almost flawless image of perfection. The truth is that never in my life have I seen as much self-deception, envy, competition, narcissism and distorted ego as I have seen among these superficial 'spiritual' types. Coaches and gurus who speak of the abundance of the universe but are jealous of the success of others. Authors who write about purity of intention and soul while they plagiarize the works of others. Mediums who talk about love and truth but do nothing but gossip and lie. Self-proclaimed guides who claim to have been put here to 'bring light' and to 'broaden our consciousness' but go about it oddly, by disapproving and judging the way other people live.

Questions for a Curious Soul

- What are your spiritual values?

- How often do you put these values to use?

- How often are you not able to live by your spiritual values?

- Do you gossip about others even though you consider it important to preserve your integrity?

- How often do you choose the victim role, even though your spiritual self knows that events come your way because you probably need them for your inner growth?

- Do you profess to believe in oneness but still find yourself behaving selfishly?

- How often do you promise something to someone and not follow through on your promise?

- How often do you lie (including lies you tell yourself) even while you say it's important to live truthfully?

The Spiritual 'Quick Fix'

Making your life *look* a bit spiritual is far easier than actually *being* spiritual. As I've said, spiritual living is not the same as talking about spirituality or thinking or reading about it. It is what you *are* and what you *do*. It is the nature of your thoughts and convictions – and the choices you make based upon them. It is wanting to examine your actions at all times, and especially during the difficult moments in your life. It is your willingness to look inside for the causes – and the solutions – instead of pointing to people, events or circumstances outside yourself. You are spiritual when you are willing to recognize and acknowledge everything you experience as your own creation – even (or especially) when what you experience is negative.

•

Spirituality calls for intellectual maturity.

•

Spirituality revolves around taking your own responsibility, and this calls for intellectual maturity. Many people find all of this just too much to deal with. Many of us would prefer to stay children as long as possible. A child who whines and cries when he doesn't get what he wants (or, rather, gets what he *doesn't* want) and keeps on blaming other people. A child who wants to eat the moment she's hungry, wants to have everything right now but doesn't want to pay the price for it or take the consequences. Most people want instant solutions for the most complex problems. This is why those call-in TV shows and phone lines with mediums or tarot readers are so popular. They offer a spiritual *quick fix* for people who are walking around with faint feelings of discontent, going around in circles and watching things in their lives go awry, yet aren't ready to look at the actual causes of those problems and so can't get interested in working on real solutions. They prefer salves for the symptoms and Band-Aids for the problems – all applied from the outside: 'When will I get that gorgeous new house or great new job? When will that perfect, everlasting love appear? Will I get enough alimony from my ex to take it easy for a while? Oh yeah, and my ex will be totally miserable, right?'

•

There's no McSpirit drive-thru for a quick bite
of spiritual fast food.

•

A good friend of mine who is a medium once worked for a short time at one of those phone helplines. Exhausted and despondent after a long day, he'd say, 'People are calling me because they want to hear from me that their lives will soon change magically for the better. They truly believe this change is going to come falling out of the sky. They don't see the correlation between the way they think and the actions they take and the effect it has on their lives.' People would often hang up on him in anger because he didn't say what they wanted to hear, but confronted them with their own responsibility. Often he would say to them, genuinely confused, 'How can you expect positive changes if you keep thinking negatively? How can you expect a constructive outcome if you keep acting in a destructive way? How do you plan to accomplish anything in life without faith or trust?'

'People want to keep making choices for the short term,' he told me, 'but they want the results of those choices to be good in the long term! For example, they cheat on their spouse for years and then ask me, "Can you tell me when we will finally be happy together?"' What he found most telling was that most people weren't calling the phone lines in order to get more self-knowledge or insight, but because they were yearning for instant solutions and cut-and-dried answers to their life questions. 'Really, so many people do not understand that from their destructive choices they can never achieve positive change. You just can't build a positive, pure life on the rubble of Ground Zero.'

We in the West live in a part of the world where we have very little to complain about. So it's no surprise that spirituality has become a trend. If all your basic needs are met but you are still dissatisfied, then it is time to shift the boundaries. But we are lazy creatures; even for the journey within we would prefer to buy the all-inclusive ticket from the travel agent. So an industry springs into motion to service our every need. They promise us mountains of gold without our having to do any of the work. Achieve a state of enlightened consciousness in one day? Sure! According to all the new gurus, it's no problem! On top of that, spirituality is being presented as a way to easily fulfil all your material dreams. (You want a Ferrari? Visualize it!) The spiritual gold-digger is an über-consumer who even goes shopping for the last remaining part of his humanity: his feelings. But sadly, there is no spiritual fast food. There is no McSpirit drive-thru with golden arches where you drive up to the window when you're hungry for a quick bite of soul. Spirituality is something that grows over the years; it comes when you are ready to face the truth – to take your own responsibility, have the discipline to keep following the road within, and be willing to surrender to all that life has to offer in all its glory.

The Advantages of Spirituality

I am no spiritual cynic or sceptic; on the contrary. In my eyes, life cannot exist without spirituality, for the simple reason that we are spiritual beings. However, I am 'spiritually critical': I only believe in real *hands-on* spirituality. I believe, and experience almost daily, that spirituality gives life inspiration, depth and meaning, but also that there is no real spirituality without discipline. Every time you are ready to use that discipline to look for the answers deep inside and incorporate them into your everyday life – to look at your life with 'spiritual eyes' (yes, even during the worst possible moments) – then a whole new world will open up for you. Because you are paying more attention to the deeper meaning of everything that you come across on your life's path, you will start to see connections between what you feel, think, dream, desire and do and the *results* that you create in your existence. This brings you peace and light, relief and freedom. Because as soon as you bring the cause-and-effect relationships to the surface, you will gain insight into what you (consciously or subconsciously) create and how you react to it. Real spiritual living means that you are willing to recognize, experience and accept that everything is *your creation*. When you truly start to make that connection, the feeling that you are helpless against outside powers and influences will dissipate. You will see that you start to align – often without even noticing – your outside world with your inside world.

Real spiritual living offers you freedom. The freedom to make different choices. To act and to think differently, and therefore to create and attract different experiences. You can only experience this freedom if you choose to accept your pain and unmet needs instead of fighting them – only if you're willing to accept your life as it is right *now*. As soon as you open yourself up to that, you will create real space for renewal and change. By accepting what is, you allow yourself to let go of the old source from which you created your life's current circumstances.

•

Everything that felt wrong in your life instantly becomes right when you become spiritual.

•

A spiritual life is a rich life. Because from the moment you start looking from the outside in and start to gain more self-knowledge, you find out what themes your soul chose for its development, and then you know what your karma is. From that point on, you will notice that all events and encounters that come your way have meaning. The relationship you have with the woman or man in your life has meaning; your disability can become meaningful, or the fact that you just lost your job. Everything, literally everything, that somehow felt as if it wasn't quite right in your life – coming from an inability to accept your experience – instantly becomes right the moment your life becomes spiritual. Just as soon as your ego accepts your karma, everything around you will have a purpose and you will understand that all events that cross your path are opportunities to develop that karma. Everything you saw as unpleasant or negative before will suddenly be full of meaning. But you are ready for this only when your ego gives up the need for control and stops arguing against what is happening in reality. This can be quite difficult, because you have to completely accept. Complete acceptance hurts, because it forces you to say goodbye to your dreams and illusions and face the fear that comes with loss of control. But behind that fear, that's where you find the space for change.

Summary

- Spirituality is absolute. You live spiritually or you don't. There is no in-between, no compromise. It is not something you do one moment and not the next. It does not have an on/off switch.

- Spiritual living takes over your whole existence, down to the smallest details. It determines the true nature of your way of life, your views, choices and actions.

- Reading, writing and talking about spirituality is one thing; applying spirituality in real life, actually doing it, is something very different.

- Making your life *look* a little spiritual is far easier than *being* spiritual in everything you do.

- Spiritual living means being willing, over and over again, to look within and discover what your unique contribution to this world can be.

- For many people, that's already too much trouble. They prefer pre-fabricated all-in-one solutions. So it's no surprise that all those call-in TV shows and phone lines with mediums and tarot readers are so successful. But there are no quick fixes in the spiritual life.

- As soon as you start looking at the world with spiritual eyes, you will sense the connection between what you feel, think, dream, desire and do and the results of this creative power in your life. You will start to see how you constantly bring your outside world – often without noticing – into alignment with your inner world.

- A spiritual life is a rich life, because it shows you that all events and encounters that come your way have meaning. Everything in your experience that you couldn't accept because it somehow didn't feel right *becomes* right the moment you become spiritual.

Chapter 6

SPIRITUALITY IS
ENDING THE SEARCH

*Do not keep searching for the truth,
just let go of your opinions.*

— BUDDHA

*H*ave you ever turned your whole house upside down on a beautiful sunny day because you misplaced your sunglasses? Even looked in the refrigerator, because they just might be in there? Only to discover they were on top of your head the whole time? This is the trouble with searching. When you search for something, you're so focused on what you want to find that you create a sort of 'consciousness vacuum' and you can no longer perceive things clearly. Admit it – isn't it a bit odd to be unaware of the fact that you have a pair of glasses on top of your head?

This is exactly the problem with searching for spirituality – or for happiness, or love, or yourself. If you are searching for something, by definition it means you believe that something is missing and that there is something you're going to find. It also means you have a preconceived notion about what you are going to find, what 'it' will be, how it will look and, most importantly, what it will bring you once you have found it. It may also be that you're a 'perpetual searcher' and you truly have no idea what it is you are searching for. But you are still driven by the conviction that you're missing *something*. And just like the sunglasses on top of your head, that missing something eludes you because you're too focused on the search to see what's right in front of you.

There are so many examples – take love. The moment someone stops looking and thinks, *OK, whatever, I am perfectly fine being alone*, suddenly that elusive perfect person appears. It's not a case of 'Seek and you shall find' – it's when you stop the seeking that you find.

◆

Be whatever it is you are seeking.

◆

Searching blinds you. As long as you are searching you are making it impossible for yourself to find. You are blinded because you have a predetermined goal, preset in your mind, that you are obsessed with. While you strive for your goal, that goal is all you see, and without even noticing, you miss important aspects of what is actually happening right before your eyes. You only *find* when you are free. Finding means being *open* to what you may find and having no predetermined goal. It means pushing aside the veil of your opinions and judgements in order to see what's really there. It means turning off the slideshow of your thoughts – all the little pictures of how your life *should* look – and seeing with an unbiased spirit, open eyes and an open heart.

Not Seeking, but Being

To me one of the most beautiful and spiritual stories ever told is *Siddhartha* by Hermann Hesse. This story, which takes place in India, is about the son of a Brahmin who, torn between worldly desires and self-denial, goes in search of the truth and his True Self. He begins a long journey into the big, bad world. As an ascetic in the mountains, he fasts and meditates, but does not find the truth that way. Roaming around as a mendicant monk, he hears talk about the Buddha, but even the sacred Master cannot give him the truth. Then he plunges into life as a more common human being and immerses himself in everything worldly. He becomes a salesman in order to win the heart of the courtesan Kamala. However, the world of luxury and wealth gives him no inspiration or peace either. He says goodbye to love, to liquor and to all his belongings, then returns to being a beggar and continues his journey.

After many years, Siddhartha makes his way back to the big river where he started his journey long ago. He meets up again with the ferryman Vasudeva. He stays there and learns from Vasudeva about the power of listening: how to listen to another person, to his own inner voice, to the sound of the river and to life itself. Finally he finds happiness, after all those years of wandering the globe, in the last place he expected: in himself, with himself, for himself.

◆

You don't need to 'find yourself',
because you are yourself, right?

◆

This story shows us clearly that we may start a journey, only to find out that we never needed to set out in the first place, because we were already there. To gain that inner feeling of peace and harmony, we do not need to travel the road outward, but the road inward. Whatever we seek, in fact we already *are*. We *are* love, we *are* spirituality, we *are* happiness. More importantly, you don't need to 'find yourself', because you already *are* yourself, right?

A Law of the Universe

We tend to see what we are looking for in everything and everyone – except in ourselves.

That is why we look for things as far removed from ourselves as possible (because everything that comes from far away is exciting and special). So we project everything we think we need onto people and things outside of us. We make others responsible for our happiness and well-being. Or we blame circumstances for our unhappiness and dissatisfaction. We do this because of two things. The first is the fact that happiness and fulfilment seem so far out of reach that we hardly experience them as a reality. And we pay no attention to the happiness at hand, because something that is so close and easily accessible cannot possibly be any good. We are often hermetically sealed off from experiencing the fulfilment of the moment because we are not present in it, in the here and now.

The second thing is lack of responsibility. You hope and dream that one day something or someone will give you what you need so that you can become happy. You hope for some kind of magical solution (or salvation) from the outside. You hope one day to stumble upon a miracle that will bring you everlasting, eternal bliss. But if you are not careful, that naive assumption will keep you prisoner. The fact is you simply cannot get that inner feeling of joy from the outside. As long as you try, you will always keep searching. Once in a while, you will probably think you may have found 'it', only to be disappointed later: disappointed in yourself, in humanity, in life, in God. Buddha said, 'The road to enlightenment is disappointment.'

We will keep dealing with disappointment until we are willing to give up the outer search and start to look inward, taking responsibility for our own happiness and our own self.

◆

The change that you seek is always in yourself.

◆

'Do you believe in God?' is a question I am often asked. I say, 'Yes, just like I believe in love.' But God – just like love, happiness and spirituality itself – is not something you can experience outside of yourself. It is not possible to recognize anything outside you that you can't already find or mirror within yourself. How will you know love and truth when you see them, if you don't recognize them as fundamental aspects of you? To put it another way, you cannot attract something that you are not. This is a universal law of creation, one that spiritual traditions have spoken of from ancient times. You cannot receive something that you are not willing or able to give.

The universe doesn't grant wishes or desires that arise out of a sense of neediness. It doesn't make unfair deals, and it can unerringly sense when you want to get something that you yourself are not about to give. It doesn't respond to what you are saying you *need*, but to what you are *giving*. Do you want love in your life? *Become* more loving. Don't go out searching for everlasting love, but decide, regardless of whether or not someone you love stays in your life, that you will stay loving. Many people, searching for God or love outside of themselves, put themselves at an ever greater distance from their own strength and responsibility. Sathya Sai Baba says, 'These days everyone is searching for Godliness. Why would you need to search for something that is already in you and with you? … Godliness is the embodiment of eternal happiness and it is present in us all. It is a sign of ignorance to go out searching for a God who is everywhere.'

This may not be exactly what you want to hear, but the key is to *be* whatever it is that you are seeking. It is to *become* what you hope to find outside yourself. All change starts on the inside; after that the things on the outside change automatically. The key to the change you seek is always found within yourself. Start there, and change will absolutely come. I have found many times in my life that as soon as I am willing to change – from within – an event or encounter will come my way to show me *how* I can change.

The Secret of Acceptance

'Have you learned anything new in the past few years?' someone asked me not long ago. 'If so, what was it?' I was allowed to name only *one* thing, they said. I had to really think for a moment. I had learned so much in the past few years. But there was one important thing that had changed me on a real, deeper level: the realization that the biggest changes take place the moment you no longer believe *things* need to change.

◆

The idea of 'working on yourself' suggests that something needs to be repaired.

◆

Questions for a Curious Soul

- How would your life be if you let go of all your ideas about what it *should* look like and how you *should* be?

- How would your life feel if you stopped comparing it to those images in your head?

- Can you imagine having no opinion about anything that takes place in your life? If not, why not?

- How does it feel when you argue against reality?

- How does it feel when you accept reality?

- How would your life be if you allowed yourself to live in a world full of people with shortcomings who make mistakes, who fall and get back up with more self-knowledge and self-realization every time?

- How would you feel if you allowed yourself to be a complete human being, to embrace your flaws completely and to keep learning from them so you could get closer to your own true nature?

- What peace would it bring you if you were able to accept yourself just as you are right now, your life as it is now and others as they are?

Does that sound passive or lazy? It isn't. I still find it a very big challenge to be open to life just as it is, without judgement. There is a big secret about acceptance. We live in a material world and get everything with thought and willpower; we think we can shape everything to our liking. We are constantly thinking ahead as to what we want from life, how we want it and when we want it; we think we can plan and arrange everything from having children to keeping our good health to life itself. We are constantly on the move; we want more today than we wanted yesterday, and we'll want even more tomorrow, and it must always be more than our neighbours have. Many Westerners use spirituality only to satisfy the ego and to get (and keep) a grip on life, because real trust in themselves, life and the universe is lacking. But our orientation towards self-conscious creating and shaping of our lives has one big disadvantage: while we are busy trying to control it all, we can pretty much count on life having something completely different in store for us, something that will bring us closer to our own being (and therefore our real happiness and true strength) than all those wishes put together. Because of our urge to meddle, interfere and control, we often miss this message, so again and again life will bring us things we aren't wishing for in order to get our attention and show us what is truly important for us.

The true challenge is to look at your life's path, and everything that has happened on it, completely without judgement. To find peace and happiness, the key is to trust that if you tune in to the greater whole and walk your life's path with the goal of becoming who you are meant to become, you will be given exactly what you need to achieve that goal. Some things will just not go your way, no matter how hard you visualize, wish or pray. That's because in life you can't always get what you want – but you *do* get what you need for your inner growth. Many milestones on your life's path have to do with karma, the intention with which your soul chose this life and the experiences (or lessons of its own choosing) that are on its agenda. We could resist this, but why would we? Nothing happens to block you; everything happens to help you become who you are meant to be. So all that remains is to do what must be done instead of trying to run away.

Want What You Have

In The *Deeper Secret* I wrote: 'You often think that you know what is good for you. But what is good for you is usually what is taking place at that moment.' In the past few years I've really started to feel how relaxing and healing it is when I realize that nothing needs to 'be made right' or 'get better' in my life. That everything that comes my way is meant for me and my life. The real challenge is embracing your path, even when you don't understand your path. In most self-help books, classes and workshops, the emphasis is on wanting things to be better, wanting things to be *different*, searching, striving, fixing and, most of all, working, working very hard on yourself instead of evolving towards total acceptance of yourself and all that is. Real spirituality is about learning to *want* what is already here, instead of trying to get your way and force reality to be what you want.

Some people ask themselves: *When will that fresh breeze blow through my life? Why can't I seem to get ahead? Why is my life and growth constantly stagnating?* This has to do with their preconceived notions of what life should be. In asking these questions, though, many of us block the natural flow of our lives. The idea of 'working on yourself' suggests that something needs to be repaired or improved for you to obtain happiness. But if you use that as your basic principle for development, you will only arrive at stagnation, because it is predicated on an idea, a concept, a thought about who you should be, how your life should look and everything that needs to be fixed (within you or around you) so you can finally live your life 'right'. In fact, it is only when you completely embrace your imperfections and limitations, accept your mistakes and allow your humanity in – rather than 'working on' or 'fixing' it – that you can truly grow. Etty Hillesum, a Jewish woman killed during World War II, wrote on December 29, 1941, in one of her journals, which were written mostly during her stay in a concentration camp: 'I am … becoming aware more and more clearly to what extent everything is part of life and must not be denied: your sadness and your fatigue as well as your exuberance, your mistakes, your superficial moments, the jealousy which you fight and the inner dishonesty which you recognize.… You carry all of them within you and must not abandon any part of your life – you have enough room to accommodate and understand it all.'

◆

Every time you think something is missing in your life,
you are just creating more room for lack.

◆

Do you experience chaos and upheaval in your life? Bring it all to a halt for a moment by pausing your thoughts. Stop the wanting, searching, having to do things. Sometimes it's not for you to want, but to let things happen. Let go of your judgement of reality. Look at your life with love and appreciation, just as it is now, and at yourself as you are now. Take a deep breath and let life in. Don't keep life at a distance with all your distractions. There is nothing to fear, deny or resist. This is your life – *right now*!

Don't Work So Hard!

One of the biggest misconceptions created by New Age thinking is that in order to be happy we have to work really hard on ourselves first, because we have obviously and dramatically lost our way. Subliminally the message is: 'You big dummy. You are not doing it right. *You* are not right. It must be done differently. It must be done better.' The truth is that there is really nothing you *must* do. You *may* experience if you wish. You *can* experience what you want. But in order to create space to truly experience (and fundamentally *be*), we have to stop thinking in terms of imperfections and seeing what is lacking. Every time you think something is missing in your life, you are just creating more room for deficiency. You know why? Because your core conviction has to do with what is 'lacking'. Because you are convinced something is missing in your life, you are actually attracting the lack. Saying, 'I'm so sad that I don't have love in my life' is not a way to attract a partner. You would be much better off saying, 'I am a loving and special human being, and I have so much to offer.'

Finding happiness has nothing to with hard work. Happiness is not about *changing* who you are now, but about *relaxing into* who you are now. Spiritual living is not a matter of fighting your patterns and convictions, controlling your thoughts and feelings. Only one thing is important: allowing reality into your world without resistance. Then your life will become real, you will become real and your encounters with others will become real. This way, you will experience more and more ease in your life. Problems will vanish into thin air (because once you have let go of your judgements about what reality is, problems don't exist). You will feel more comfortable in your body, you will have more energy and you will look better. You will elevate yourself to a completely different vibration frequency, and you will notice that people respond to you differently. It's quite possible you will suddenly (and seemingly by coincidence) come across the very people and opportunities you need and things will become much easier altogether. This happens because, when you accept life just as it is, you are taking down a huge road-block and allowing the energy to flow and pass freely. By accepting what is, you stop blocking your life.

•

Happiness is not found by changing who you are now; happiness comes from relaxing into who you are now.

•

You can find peace and freedom only when you allow reality into your world. Not resisting, but being open to all that is, without judgement. Not putting the emergency brake on your life, but letting life move naturally. People always strive for happiness, and they think that happiness equals the mere absence of problems. So, when problems still present themselves (and how could they not?), they try to avoid them, fight them or resolve them. We ask ourselves far too often: *How can I change something about this situation or relationship?* We should really be asking ourselves: *What is the best position I can take in this situation?* Letting the problems be what they are, and seeing them as a real part of life instead of trying to fight them, does not make us passive, fatalistic people. On the contrary, surrendering to reality is a very proactive approach to life. Without fear, and with an open heart, you let life in. Without judgement, but with curiosity, you await the future. Then, in everything that happens, you will find a glimpse of glory, truth and beauty – a glimpse of the holy – no matter what the circumstances.

Summary

- Searching can blind you. As long as you search, you make it impossible for yourself to find anything. While you are chasing your goal, you only have eyes for that goal, and so you may be missing what's happening right before you.

- You only find when you are completely free. Finding means being open and having no preset goal. It means seeing through the veil of your opinions and judgements for a clear view of reality.

- With this approach, many of us block the flow of our lives, subconsciously resisting change. The concept of 'working on yourself' suggests that something needs to be fixed or improved. It is geared towards an idea of who you should be and how your life should look. If you use this as your starting point, you will only stagnate instead of developing more.

- Spiritual living is not a question of getting your thoughts or feelings under control. Finding happiness has nothing to do with hard work. It is not about fighting your patterns and convictions. It is about only one thing: letting reality into your life without resistance.

- When you let reality in, you will find much more relaxation and ease coming into your life too. You will feel better in your body, be more energetic and look better. You will elevate yourself to a completely different vibration frequency, and you will notice that people respond to you differently.

- When you let reality in, you will find peace and freedom in any circumstances. You will find glimpses of the holy in everything that happens.

- Most self-help books, classes and workshops place too much emphasis on searching, striving, fixing and 'working on yourself' instead of accepting yourself and all that is happening in reality.

Chapter 7

SPIRITUALITY IS TAKING EVERY CHANCE FOR GROWTH

Teachers come in all forms and disguises.

— ELISABETH KÜBLER-ROSS

'*L*ife is a mirror.' Could you imagine a more predictable spiritual one-liner than that?

No, I didn't think so. Good reason to keep reading. Because labelling ideas 'predictable' or 'cliché' is an inventive way to water truth down and to avoid taking action. Saying you've 'heard it all before' is a trick for people who tend to live in their heads (meaning they would rather contemplate than participate in life) to keep life at bay and avoid any true self-realization.

When I once asked someone what he thought of a certain spiritual book with a very surprising view on a well-known subject, he answered: 'Well, what can I say? We've pretty much heard all of that before – been there, done that.' Bam! In a split second, what do we have here? A giant self-sabotage mechanism! Which, by the way, we all have in us – me too and, yeah, you too. Intellectually, at the level of understanding things in the brain, hearing or reading about something is very different from actually *living* it down to the smallest details. So the question is not 'Are you familiar with this idea?' but 'What are you *doing* with it?'

Clichés ('If you don't love yourself, you cannot love others') don't become clichés for no reason; they often contain deep spiritual wisdom. They are little gifts that we all too readily discard – precisely because they sound so predictable to us. Yet I still see many intelligent people, even people with 'spiritual knowledge', avoiding the truth about themselves. Especially people who are used to explaining things intellectually and unravelling everything with their minds; they often have developed this self-sabotage mechanism to a high degree. Once you *understand* an idea, there seems to be no pressing reason to allow the information already in your head to travel down and penetrate your heart, where you can truly *do* something with it.

•

Spirituality is rooted in the earth, not in your head.

•

OK, next example: 'People and events mirror the things we have to attend to in ourselves.' I will not ask you, 'Do you understand this?' because I think anyone reading this book has some understanding of this concept. A more useful question would be 'How often do you succeed in using this truth (or cliché, if you prefer) in your everyday life? How has this become a real and integrated part of the way you live?' Self-development-land is filled with people who are experts in the principles and fluent in the jargon. They know exactly what it's all about. But the moment they actually have a confrontation with someone, or experience a disappointment in reality, they are the first to lose their grip – to get defensive, blame the other, be angry or literally run away from the situation. So here's another fun question: 'Why is it that you do not apply what you know?' Or, to put it another way, 'Why is it that you know exactly what to do when it doesn't matter much, but in the crucial moments you seem to experience a consciousness blackout?'

Rejection Is a Redirection

One of my best friends, Percy Dens, who is a coach and the author of the book *Business as Unusual*, a clear and thought-provoking take on spirituality in business, has this to say: 'When you know what is true, but do not act accordingly, then fear is your only motivation.' About this fear, he says: 'As people we are all addicted to validation. If someone doesn't give us what we want or need, then we feel rejected. When we don't get what we want or need from life, then we feel short-changed. "You see?" we say. "I'm not good enough; it's just not in the cards for me." Or: "You see, I don't deserve it, I am always unlucky!" But what we see as a rejection is often no more than a *redirection*, or a clue that we are on the wrong road, literally and figuratively. People and circumstances mirror the things within us of which we aren't fully conscious yet. Problems in relationships with others point to unresolved issues in our own psyche. They tell us a lot about our shortcomings and what we should be doing about them. In order to see this more clearly, we have to, in the first place, create more space for reality, for our existence just as it is. Spirituality is rooted in the earth, not in your head. Insights that don't influence actions are a mere semblance of changed thinking, unless we take the advice that Oprah has given to her audience at the end of her show: "Now that you *know* better, you will *do* better!""

Spiritual Living Is a Decision

Cliché or not, life *is* a mirror in which you can see all the various aspects of yourself. Encounters, events and circumstances are a reflection of your inner landscape. This also means that life as we experience it is a direct reflection of how we think about ourselves and what we wish for ourselves. For years I have been fascinated by the subjects of self-worth, self-respect and self-compassion and have written about them extensively. In my first book, *I Love Me*, I pointed out how we create a large part of the outside world from our inside world, and how therefore our self-image is often our fate. We continuously create a life for ourselves that reflects what we think we are worth, and form our positions according to circumstances or events that work for or against us.

•

What we are is what we attract.

•

Looking at things this way is not a gift but a decision. It is the decision to take responsibility instead of walking away. Before you can make that decision, you have to be willing to get to know the real you and to use everything that happens to you in the outside world as a GPS to navigate your inner landscape. This is a decision that you make not once, but over and over again, every single day. Whether you are going to work, a birthday party or lunch with a colleague, if you *decide* to see yourself in everything that comes your way that day, then you will.

A whole new world will open to those who dare to see their circumstances in this light. It could be that you think you are living a very conscious life, but you don't see that you are still treating yourself and others the way you were treated as a child. That you *allow* yourself to be treated in a way you recognize from your youth. That you attract damaged people because you have not healed what is damaged in you. Or that you damage people (no matter how subtle, indirect or concealed the damage) because you are damaged yourself. If, for example, you have unresolved issues with your father or mother, it is likely that you attract relationships and people who bring out this issue in you, giving the adult a chance to try to resolve this issue inside.

Of course, the problem is that because those old patterns and concepts *are* so familiar, they are difficult to break through. It is logical that in a confrontation your reflex is to try to escape it (by rationalizing, anger, accusations, blame or needing to be right); after all, you are being asked to look at your inner reality, and for most of us – when it comes down to it – this is not an easy task.

Everyone's life is the way it is because this is what we believe about our lives in this moment. Our relationships are what they are because of what we believe we deserve or need. So here I go again – I have said this in previous books, but it is so important to absorb this fully: *You attract people and experiences like a magnet towards yourself that reflect your exact subconscious needs, desires, doubts and fears.* What we are and what we radiate is what we attract. When someone else's behaviour irritates or frustrates us, it says nothing about the True Self of the other person, but it says everything about *our* self. The irritation and frustration are our feelings, and they have nothing to do with anyone else. Only we are responsible for the state of our consciousness, and only we can make a real change in our situation. The other person is only a mirror in which we can see ourselves. The more insight we gain, the easier it gets to see the places within us that certain relationships – or problems in relationships – come from.

Don't Resist, Engage

When you find yourself facing difficulty or unpleasantness, don't run away from it. Instead, throw yourself completely into the situation that caused it so you can learn from it. Throwing yourself into a situation completely means not criticizing what's happening, not resisting it but engaging with it. You can have your own thoughts about things, but make sure they are contemplative instead of judgemental. Use circumstances to get more insight into yourself. Know what the themes of your soul's development are, and leave others out of it. They have their own life lessons, which they will learn at their own speed and in their own way.

◆

You don't have to travel to Tibet or India to find a guru. Life itself is your greatest teacher.

◆

Once you decide to see events and encounters as 'medicine' to heal yourself, it does not mean that suddenly your boss is no longer a power-hungry idiot, or that your friend suddenly understands what he could not understand before, or that your relationship with your mother-in-law is suddenly perfect. *Your* view will change how *you* experience the situation, but you should know that others are (and are certainly allowed to be) the same as they were before. Marianne Williamson says in *The Age of Miracles*: 'God's intention is that [we] heal each other's wounds....

Whoever is willing to do the work in a relationship, seeing it as their own opportunity for self-healing, will receive the blessing whether the other person makes the same choice or not. And, ultimately, all of us will get there; lessons we haven't learned will just keep coming around until we do.'

Your Guru Is Life Itself

In order to meet interesting gurus, you don't need to travel to Tibet or India. Life itself is by far the greatest teacher (and much closer at hand): the partner who sits at the dinner table with you and sleeps next to you every night, your child, brother or sister, mother or father, colleague, maid, nanny, best friend or neighbour, or the cleaner who came by your hospital room. Your teachers come in disguise and present themselves in the most ordinary settings.

Some of them show you where your boundaries are, not by who they are but by what function they serve in that moment for your growth. That function might be to encourage you, to help you towards insight, to teach you to voice your opinion and set boundaries, or some-

Questions for a Curious Soul

- The next time you find yourself in a situation you would rather avoid, can you ask yourself: *What can I learn from this situation? What message is being sent to me?*

- What, at this moment, do you think is the recurring theme of your inner growth?

- What lesson that you need to learn is mirrored in your loved one? What about the other people with whom you have a special connection, in a positive or negative sense?

- What is the true function of your relationship for your personal growth? Do you think it serves the same function for your partner?

- What circumstances and types of people are recurring patterns in your life?

- What qualities can you develop in yourself in order to break through these patterns? For example, is it time to become more selfish (in a healthy way) and learn to set boundaries? Or is it time to make more room for the reality of someone else, to ease up on your boundaries and open your heart more?

times to give you a wake-up call. This means that you may learn the most important truths about yourself from the people you 'hate' (or to whom you feel the most resistance). It is not only your romantic partner who comes with lessons for you. There's no such thing as coincidence in the universe. Friend or enemy, acquaintance or stranger, whoever appears on your life's stage comes with a message or a lesson.

You're allowed to run away from them, and from the situations where you confront them, for as long as you like. But don't forget that your soul has been waiting for these messages for a long time. Besides, while you're busy running away, it's not as if those lessons will just disappear. They will follow you around and confront you over and over with whatever it is you are not doing – or with what you are doing and shouldn't be. They will keep changing their shape and appearance, but bring the same message each time until you have taken care of business. Have you ever noticed, for example, that sometimes over the course of a whole week (or month or year) you keep getting, in a variety of ways, through different people and seemingly coincidental situations, the same lesson handed to you?

•

You're allowed to run away from your teachers,
but the lessons won't just disappear.

•

Those are important moments, because that is when you are being asked for some hard-core transformation. When a lot of crazy things are happening back to back in your life, you may ask yourself: *When is this ever going to end?!* But you could also step back and look at the common denominator in all these events. Even though it may *seem* as if they are all separate and unrelated problems, they still – and I have experienced this myself many times – represent the same lesson. So instead of thinking, *Why is this all so difficult?* you could take the road of spiritual development and say to yourself, *I find life a bit difficult at the moment because a lot is being asked of me – so I guess life is in a hurry with me!* Lama Lobsang told me that Tibetans actually pray for problems. 'Problems on our path show us we are ready for growth,' he said. 'Some people reach eighty years old, but have never experienced much, because they were not ready. Therefore we bless our difficulties, because it is a privilege to be able to grow and have the opportunity to work on our karma.' I am sure you have felt at one point or another that you're avoiding certain lessons. That you are dragging your feet, quietly hoping to put the whole thing off, while on the inside you know the moment will come when you will have to face it anyway. You probably also recognize the feeling of relief and total freedom after you have taken on the confrontation and got past your resistance and fear. And you may have noticed that as soon as you acted according to what you knew (deep inside) and did what had to be done, positive things started to happen and things started moving in your life that had been stuck up to that point.

◆

Your teachers come in disguise and present themselves to you in the most ordinary settings.

◆

If we endlessly delay by avoiding our lessons, then we are holding back our own progress and also, without noticing it, often blocking the good things that are waiting for us. But when you recognize and acknowledge your lessons, then you break the 'karmic spell', which means you won't end up in the same situation again. Then the *next* karmic set of events and encounters will start to take shape so you can take the next step in your spiritual growth and continue balancing out your karma.

Breaking the Spell

In many ways, life is a lot like the movie *Groundhog Day* – the hilarious film about a guy named Phil, a cranky weatherman (played by Bill Murray) from a local TV station who against his will travels to a small town to report on the day the groundhog sees (or doesn't see) its shadow, a folksy way of predicting how long the winter will be. I have seen this movie so many times, and it is still one of my all-time favourites because it explains, in a very simple way, exactly how karma works.

Phil the weatherman gets trapped in a kind of time warp. When he tries to go home that evening after the broadcast, a giant snowstorm forces him and his team to stay in the small town. The next morning he awakens, only to find out it is the previous day all over again: Groundhog Day. He hears exactly the same jokes and exactly the same songs on the radio. On the street he sees the same people, and they say the same things. Everything that happened the day before is happening all over again. Much to his chagrin, he must also do the same dreaded report all over again. The next morning he wakes up at the same time, in the same place, on the same day again: Groundhog Day.

•

*When you decide to look at things differently,
your world will change.*

•

It soon becomes clear to Phil that he is the only one stuck in this time warp and that other people have no idea it's happening. Every day he finds new ways to get around doing his television report. He hits on all the women, and if it doesn't work, the next day he just tries a new approach, because everyone else has forgotten anyway. Boredom leads him to try crazy experiments, like jumping off tall buildings. But he still wakes up the next morning on … Groundhog Day.

At a certain point he has really had enough of the endless repetition – enough of himself – and he decides to start looking at things and doing things differently. He decides to help a homeless man whom he had previously ignored and left to his own devices, and he also helps some other people in need, which makes him suddenly appreciate them more. Eventually, one day, Phil is able to prevent every single accident in the small town, since he knows when they are going to happen. Even his news story, which he's been rushing through, suddenly becomes a work of art. The woman he tried so hard to get now comes to him because he's become so much more pleasant to be with. At that moment, the time warp ends and Phil is finally able to leave the small town if he wants to. But now he doesn't feel so driven to leave. His resistance to reality has receded, and as far as he's concerned things are good just the way they are. He has completely accepted what is, and within that reality he has done the best he could and what he felt had to be done. Once he is finally able to escape from the town, escape is no longer necessary. He decides not to return to the city he came from, but chooses instead to settle down with his new love in the town he had so loathed before he came, which now he doesn't want to leave.

We will all be playing the same scenes over and over again in our lives, going around in circles and keeping ourselves prisoners in time, until we make a decision to do it the 'other' way. That's when we truly learn our lesson. When you decide to look at things differently, your world will change. That is what living spiritually means. It is not about searching for changes outside of yourself, but making changes on the inside, which changes your relationship with everything happening around you. The stress at work, the complications of your relationship … Decide to look at everything differently – you may surprise yourself!

Summary

- People and events mirror the things we need to deal with in ourselves.

- Like a magnet, you attract experiences and relationships that coincide with your subconscious needs, desires, doubts and fears.

- When a situation becomes difficult or unpleasant, don't run away – throw yourself into the situation completely so you can learn from it. Stepping into a situation completely means stopping your resistance to reality – not criticizing it, but accepting it.

- Others show you where your boundaries are, not by who they are but by what function they serve at that moment to further your growth. This means that you can learn the most important truths about yourself from the people you resist or even hate.

- There's no such thing as coincidence in the universe. Friend or enemy, acquaintance or stranger, whoever appears on the stage of your life comes with a lesson for you – a message your soul may have been waiting a very long time for.

- Looking at things this way is not a gift but a decision –
  the decision to take responsibility instead of running
  away. Before you can make that decision, you must
  be willing to get to know yourself and use everything
  happening outside of yourself as a GPS guide into
  your inner landscape.

Chapter 8

SPIRITUALITY IS LISTENING TO THE VOICE OF YOUR SOUL

If only I listened to my own rhythm,
and tried to live in accordance with it.
Much of what I do is mere imitation,
springs from a sense of duty or from preconceived
notions of how people should behave.
The only certainties about what is
right and wrong are those that spring
from sources deep inside oneself.

— ETTY HILLESUM

*I*n everyone's life – sooner or later – there comes a moment when deep inside you feel it is time for transformation. Time for a new 'life strategy'. Time to look *within*. That moment comes when you realize that you seem to keep ending up in the exact same place in your relationship, in your job or with your weight or health. Maybe you are experiencing such a moment right now in which you're getting a little (or very) tired of yourself. That is a good thing. Nothing is as good as feeling *I'm sick and tired of being sick and tired* – as if you're beginning to repeat yourself and your life as it is now is weighing on you. These are the moments when you make a shift in consciousness. You suddenly see the pattern you are caught in. You suddenly see yourself behave or react in a way that lets you know: *This is old behaviour, this is over, I don't need it anymore; if I continue doing this, I will keep ending up in the same place, and by now I know this place all too well – I am done looking at this landscape.*

Being tired of yourself and your existence as it is today, and maybe even being depressed about it, are signs that your soul needs to be acknowledged and heard. Most people feel the need to run away from that feeling as fast as possible, to stay busy, to never be alone, to eat and drink too much – to do everything they possibly can not to confront the emptiness and chaos within them. Many people raise going around in circles to an art form; anything is better than travelling the real road inward. But this way, life becomes more occupational therapy than a glorious journey through earthly existence. It keeps you busy and off the streets, but it has very little to do with self-realization and with the magic of being human.

•

Why are we so quick to silence the voice of our soul?

•

When I say 'going round in circles', I also mean avoiding the emptiness, the chaos or the depression by running off to a psychologist for a heart-to-heart talk, or to the doctor for a little pill, or to as many spiritual teachers and healers as you can fit in. Think about it: what exactly needs to be *healed* in that moment? Why take someone out of his or her natural development process? Why are we always so quick to silence the voice of our soul?

I once read that 1 out of 16 people in Holland takes antidepressants. Are you as surprised as I am? Doesn't this suggest that we have lost our way? I am not saying that medication can't be helpful for people in extreme cases who are mentally suffering. I would never judge the use of drugs for someone who suffers from a serious psychological condition. But 1 in 16 people on Prozac – surely those can't *all* be serious cases?

I'm concerned, to say the least, that we are trying to protect ourselves with pills from the natural flow of life. Life is a constant cycle of beginnings and endings, renewal and change. Those cycles coincide with saying good-bye to old hopes and dreams, old thought patterns and convictions. Saying good-bye to the old to make way for the new is the essence of letting go. Yes, letting go means temporarily losing your grip, it can cause fear, and … it hurts. So what? Whoever said that life should be without pain?

●

This is spirituality:
things don't have to get better in order to be good.

●

Pain gives us structure in life, connects us to the absolute depth of human existence. Every major transition in life, as well as illness or a sudden disability, can go hand in hand with what seems a temporary mental 'breakdown' – exhaustion, panic, confusion and marked mood changes. These are the dark nights of the soul that we all experience sooner or later – in a variety of ways. They can lead to a fundamentally different way of looking at life; they invite us to become who we really are. They are almost always turning points that can give our life so much more meaning if we let them. So we shouldn't medicate those dark nights away with pills. They are transitional moments, deep initiations that lead us to the secret of truly *being*!

Don't Medicate Life Away!

The 'problem pill' business is a billion-dollar industry worldwide. Many of us try very hard to live life as painlessly as possible and to return things to 'normal' as quickly as possible after any disruption. 'The parameters for the use of antidepressants have been stretched to the limit,' says the spokesperson for a Dutch organization for people with a psychiatric disorder. 'We have started taking it more lightly. The issues we use to consider part of the "normal suffering" in life we now prescribe pills for.'

◆

We have nothing to gain from suppressing the unavoidable pain that life brings.

◆

When life becomes difficult for a moment, if it doesn't go the way we planned, we just take a little pill. This means that many people are living in a constant state of fear and avoidance instead of a place of growth and development. As soon as life takes us in a different direction from the one we set out in, or we feel different than we're used to feeling, we do everything we can to get things back to how they were before, to reset life to the old familiar settings we are used to. But our soul doesn't need to return to the old way. It is far more concerned with using everything that happens in our lives as an opportunity to become *new*! The famous psychotherapist and philosopher Thomas Moore writes in *Dark Nights of the Soul*: 'Familiarity can bring you tranquillity, but you also need the sting and chaos of the new. To be alive entails both of these qualities, the yin and yang of peace and pain.'

The ease with which we take a pill when we think we have lost our grip on things – or on our very self – stems from a number of assumptions we make about life:

1. Good fortune is the same as the absence of problems.

2. We have a universal right to happiness and mental health, which, if all else fails, we can claim from our family doctor by way of a prescription.

3. We should get medication prescribed to us for self-transformation.

4. We can grow without going through life's unavoidable phases of fear, doubt and pain.

5. The darkness is something we should fear and battle against or something we need to be 'cured' of.

All these assumptions are wrong. We are not crazy; there is nothing wrong with us. Not when we are in balance, not when we are out of balance. That's what spirituality means: something doesn't by definition have to get better in order to be good. There is only 'something wrong' when we try to banish the unavoidable pain all people experience, when we put the emergency brake on life and keep real experience at a distance. We fear making mistakes or falling off the wagon. We fear what may come if we let the chaos in, if we take a moment to really examine our inner contradictions. We fear all that may come to the surface if we listen to the voice of our soul and face the darkness in ourselves.

But finding your own path, becoming who you really are, is a matter of trial and error. It is important to understand that night and day are indissolubly connected to each other the same way that doubt and pain are part of life. We have nothing to gain from suppressing the unavoidable pain that life brings. Pain is a wake-up call from our soul! Pain is the road map; it can guide us to the parts of ourselves that are asking for attention, acceptance, love and healing. So pain should not be suppressed or defended against, but allowed in and understood in all its glory!

How Do You Know the Voice of Your Soul?

Physically we are born only once, but the soul experiences an eternal, never-ending rebirth. The soul works in a constant cycle of renewal and progress towards something, so the trick is to find out what that something is in your current life. What is the goal your soul chose in this life? What does it have planned? Why did it choose this specific life and these circumstances?

What does your soul want to learn? What is it contributing? In other words, what is the purpose of your life on earth?

◆

The voice of your soul is always calm, determined and decisive.

◆

You may be thinking, *I have no idea!* No worries – most people have no idea. For years I had no idea either. Many people I speak to say: 'Living an inspired and passionate life sounds intriguing, but I don't understand how to get there!' Well, it's not as complicated as it may sound. Listening to your inner voice, being connected to your passion and your life goal, is not reserved for higher life forms. It's not as pretentious as it sounds, either. It's just a matter of not suppressing your inner voice, but rather encouraging its existence. Don't suppress it with a pill, a glass of wine, too much (or not enough) food, shopping, golf, jogging or bicycle racing. Certainly not by running to a new spiritual workshop, medium, chakra healer or aura doctor every time you feel a little 'off'. When you start taking yourself seriously, then you are taking your feelings seriously. But pay attention: by *feelings* I mean something very different from *emotions*. Your emotions arise from your thinking and belong to the agenda and voice of your ego; they come and go. The voice of your soul is always present. Do you want to know how to tell the difference between the two? The voice of your soul always addresses you calmly, is always determined and decisive. The voice from deep within doesn't speak through your intellect, but through your feelings, which are the language of your soul. In *Entering the Castle*, Caroline Myss says of learning to recognize the difference between the voices of the imagination, the ego and the soul: 'Your intuition is relentless and cannot be budged from its position whereas the ego can be talked into or out of anything.'

Questions for a Curious Soul

- When was the last time you received a clear, intuitive 'heavy hitter' of a message about yourself, your life or your situation?

- Did you listen to your inner voice in that situation? What happened?

- When was the last time you ignored a hunch? What thought did you use to silence your inner voice? What was the result?

- Why do you resist your inner guidance? What are you afraid of? What do you think you will gain?

- In those instances, are you tempted to put the blame on others?

- Are you afraid of change? Take a good, hard look at whether – and how – you may be blocking change and growth subconsciously by tuning out your inner voice.

How 'Soul Smart' Are You?

Are you someone who is often unaware of what you are feeling? If so, you're certainly not alone. We all live chaotic and demanding lives in this society. If we are not careful, life takes over and it seems as if we're on a high-speed train we can't get off. We are being guided by forces from the outside instead of taking the wheel and taking directions from the inside. We have convinced ourselves there is no other way to be – that otherwise our house of cards will collapse! But is that really true?

◆

Emotion, rationality and spirituality don't act in opposition to each other, but in service of each other.

◆

Recognizing, let alone welcoming, your feelings in the midst of the chaos of your daily life is incredibly difficult. However, it's in your deepest feelings that your highest truth is hidden. The challenge is to get down to the nitty-gritty of those feelings without turning your whole life upside down – because most of the time that is not really necessary. Simply living your daily life is by far the best way to practise hearing and recognizing your inner voice. Your inner being calls your attention to feelings, dreams, passions and insights. Those feelings and perceptions are so pure and clear, such intuitive 'heavy hitters', that they are very difficult to ignore. But often that's exactly what we do – we ignore them.

As I was writing this chapter, a good friend of mine from Belgium came by for a visit. He has an international business in packing machines. The story he told me clearly shows how our inner voice constantly announces things we need to change and how we ignore those hunches when we aren't ready to see the truth. My friend and his business partner had started a joint venture with a company whose managing director had shown himself to be an unkind and unreliable man. Not surprisingly, big problems developed. 'Didn't you feel that this man could not be trusted?' I asked my friend. Of course he had. 'In fact,' he said, 'I even thought that if I came across a person like that in my daily life, I would turn and walk in the other direction. When I looked him in the eye, I instantly felt I couldn't trust him. But then you go home and think about it, even when you feel the signals very clearly, and think: *Well, maybe I misjudged him. I'm sure it will be all right.'*

•

It's much better to be rejected for being who you are than to be accepted for being who you're not.

•

But it wasn't all right, and now the business was in trouble. That's how it goes all the time, don't you agree? Every day, perhaps many times a day, our inner voice reminds us of the need for change, warns us to use the utmost caution, encourages us to be braver or challenges us to show more willpower. But because we lack self-knowledge (and, therefore, lack real trust – after all, a self you don't know is a self you cannot trust), we still put the absolute, ever-present, pure knowledge of our inner being aside, reason it away and stick our heads more firmly in the sand. Staying in denial about any part of our lives is dangerous.

Not that reason isn't useful. I am a very rational person myself. Emotion, rationality and spirituality don't act in opposition to each other, but in service of each other. When it comes to the essential things in my life, though, I listen *only* to the voice of my soul and see *only* with the eyes of my heart. Reason is a good toolbox, but not much more than that. The most important aspects of human beings, the truths of the heart and soul, cannot be recreated in a lab and will not be scientifically proven or intellectually reasoned with. Besides, our feelings never fail us, but our intellect will. Joseph Joubert said it nicely: 'Our intellect can tell us what to avoid; the heart can tell us what to do.'

◆

Our intellect may fail us, but our feelings never will.

◆

To be 'soul smart' requires following your own inner compass and not being led by your ego or your circumstances. You have to connect with your soul, hear and recognize its voice and trust it completely. Truly listening to other people, allowing their full reality in, takes practice, and it's precisely the same with your own inner voice. Truly listening to someone else is a sign of genuine interest in that person. With listening to your inner voice it is the same. Being completely open to your inner voice means that you are willing to get to know all of yourself and that you respect your own absolute, indivisible, insurmountable inner knowledge.

Being 'Soul Smart' Means:

- That you accept yourself, love life and walk your own path.

- That you don't depend on the validation or approval of others.

- That being 'just you' is enough, all you need.

- That you can be selfish (in a healthy way), see others for what they are and wish them only the best.

- That you have no need to prove your own worth by arm-wrestling with others.

- That you don't feel the need to talk about 'spirituality' or how spiritual you are; you already radiate that depth, passion, happiness, peace and enthusiasm for life.

- That by being yourself you can inspire others to get closer to who they really are.

Peace out of Chaos

My life has changed drastically over the past few years. My personal life has become fuller, with my partner, Robin, his daughter, our dogs, family and friends. My books have been published internationally. Life is busier than ever before, but at the same time richer and more peaceful than ever. My life is more peaceful because I am in a more peaceful place. Life, regardless of the busy schedule, is far less chaotic then it ever was because I do not allow any other captains on my ship; I listen to no other voice than the voice of my soul. Taking this stance may mean that people find you hard to follow, hard to accept or just plain not nice. Well, too bad. That is the natural result of listening to the voice of your soul. As a good friend told me once (and this is a good one to remember when you're on the point of abandoning yourself in order to please someone else): 'Annemarie, life is not a popularity contest. It is far better to be rejected for being who you really are than to be accepted for who you are not.'

Do you want more peace? Become more peaceful. It's really just as easy as it sounds. Do you want it now? Do it now. Take a deep breath, take a step back and reflect on how, with your intellect, you keep silencing your soul's voice – and how you keep the vicious circle of chaos going. This kind of self-reflection is crucial to making contact with your inner voice.

When I was younger I had a girlfriend who made inner chaos into an art form. 'You may not be able to walk,' she would say to me every time she had another meltdown, 'but I don't have peace of mind, and that's even worse!' I think she may have been right. There is nothing worse than feeling as if you have no peaceful home within yourself. *Why, after so many years, is there still no peace in my life?* some people ask themselves. Maybe you do too. Then it could be that, without realizing it, you're deeply attached to this very unrest and chaos in your life.

This was the case with my girlfriend. She had a very healthy and conscious lifestyle, but for every healthy thing she did, she would make, with mathematical precision, just as many self-destructive choices. She could, for example, have a visit with her Ayurvedic doctor in the morning, then in the evening down two bottles of wine. The next day she'd bicycle miles out of her way to get the very best biological salicornia and unpasteurized apple cider vinegar in order to give herself a cleansing. She became the biggest raw-food advocate I have ever encountered, and even put chlorella ice cubes in all her drinks, but she was addicted to cheese fondue and large pieces of grilled meat. She was a true master in every imaginable diet, detox and fasting programme, and she regularly did the internal colon cleanse, only to race home and dive into her refrigerator. 'Sweetie, you'll never believe what I am doing,' she'd say on the phone with her mouth full. 'I just got in from the colon-cleansing clinic, and I'm standing here with my coat still on, devouring a huge chunk of cheese.'

•

As long as you enable chaos in your life,
you have no time to listen to your inner voice.

•

With all her contradictions, she certainly was a very vibrant and entertaining friend. But for herself, she was exhausting. Because how could she find peace if she kept up her constant cycle of chaos? Of course all of us have inner contradictions; we also keep the chaos in our lives if at some point we don't come to some sort of understanding about it.

Test Your Inner Contradictions

- You want peace but continue to create unrest or allow the unrest of others into your life.

- You say you have trust but live in constant self-doubt and insecurity.

- You have convinced yourself that you live a very conscious and spiritual life, but, much like my friend, you seem to get stuck in the outer manifestations and superficial signs of spiritual things, and in reality you are doing very little to deepen your consciousness.

As long as you continue to enable chaos, you have no time to listen to your inner voice, and you are avoiding (or actively blocking) any and all development. You are going through life *troubleshooting*. You don't grant yourself peace, and therefore you don't allow for progress and growth. This is, for many people, what they stand to 'gain' from living in constant chaos: as long as there is chaos, you don't have to face the confrontation with yourself.

Connecting in the Silence

I really love silence, literal silence. It's no coincidence that Robin and I live in the middle of nature, enveloped and hidden in all that green. We have our own 'Zen ranch'. All we hear are birds and all we see are horses and sheep and deer drinking water from the reservoir on our land. At night it is totally silent and completely dark, and that peace is wonderful and healing.

In silence, you can feel in a very pure way how you would like to develop your life.

Spirituality means listening to the voice of your soul, which will help you find your way in life. By finding and expressing your True Self, you will find happiness. Every person who does this, finding his or her true nature, will make a positive difference in the world. None of this has to do with following particular spiritual 'rules', but with following your inner compass and the guidance of your inner voice. And you need silence in order to hear it. Silence reveals the True Self and allows us to get to know who we really are. The silence lets you connect with the inner intelligence of your body and enables you to get a good hard look at your life's important themes. In the silence, you can feel in a very pure way how you would like to develop your life, and you can find the inner strength to take your own authentic, 'soul smart' road.

So it's important to look at how you relate to the silence. Do you like being alone? Or do you tend to avoid your own company? In order to get to know someone, we need to spend quality time with him or her. The same goes for our own inner being. How can we get to know ourselves if we never spend any time with ourselves and are never alone with ourselves? If you are used to leading a hectic and chaotic existence, being in your own company can seem surreal and the silence can even feel threatening. Many people are deathly afraid of the silence. Afraid of the silence around them, the silence in their heads, hearts and bodies. To be spiritually receptive and to get in contact with your essence, you will have to overcome your fear.

Silence is allowing yourself to be empty, bringing the thinking to a halt, letting go and releasing the chaos – which usually has nothing to do with the literal chaos you may experience at work and in your various commitments. What does it have to do with, then, you may wonder? It has to do with our inability to be present in the here and now. Being in silence, then, is not the same as simply not speaking. So-called silent retreats should just be called 'no talking retreats'. A friend who'd done a retreat once told me, 'You wouldn't believe all the thoughts that raced through my head that week. Simply not speaking is not the same as being quiet in your head, heart and soul.' At first, finding the silence will probably not bring you the kind of peace you may have expected. In the beginning, as my friend found, your mind will not stop; it will overwhelm you with thoughts. Real inner peace is a real spiritual achievement.

In other words, learning to listen to the voice of your soul is not something you can do in two weeks. Being silent on the inside takes time, practice, discipline. It has nothing to do with taking 'silent walks' with hundreds of people at once; it is something that happens when you create a structure and make room for it in your regular everyday life, a space where you can spend time with yourself. The more you seek out the silence, the more easily your body and spirit will surrender to it.

Silence isn't something you learn from spiritual classes, and you cannot find it outside of yourself. It is about finding more peace within you. It has nothing to do with appearing to be 'in balance' or 'at peace' on the outside. That certainly can be a sign of absolute inner peace, but often it's not. I know plenty of people who are crazy, funny and entertaining on the outside; they speak fast and with passion. Yet I know they are people who are completely themselves and totally aligned with the structure of their soul. The fact that their demeanour may come across as chaotic does not mean that they have abandoned their inner silence – their True Self, their Buddha nature, the connection with their soul, whatever you want to call it – in those moments. Conversely, the people who seem most peaceful, the 'always in balance' people, often turn out to have the most chaos and unrest on the inside.

◆

*Silence is allowing yourself to be empty,
releasing the chaos, hearing the voice of your soul.*

◆

So it usually works by opposites: lively, passionate, expressive people are actually in good contact with their true, calm nature, and the even-keeled, quiet types seem to be far removed from any contact with their soul. Being busy and hectic in a healthy way can only come from a core of inner calm that's already in place. Robin and I did not choose the place where we live to 'escape' from the chaos and find silence; we chose this house because we already had our inner peace and silence. We found a home with the same 'vibration frequency' as ours! Do you understand the difference? My best friend, Percy, invariably says to the people he coaches, 'We never get tired or stressed from something happening *outside* of us, but we get tired of what happens *inside* of us.' That is so true, and the opposite is also true: we never find peace in something *outside* of ourselves, we find it by becoming more peaceful *inside*.

Summary

- Getting tired of yourself and your existence as you know it now, maybe even being depressed, are all signs that your soul needs to be heard and acknowledged. Many people have the urge to run away from that feeling as fast as possible.

- When you take yourself seriously, then you are taking your feelings seriously. Feelings aren't the same as emotions. Your emotions, which stem from your thinking and speak in the voice of your ego, come and go. But the voice of your soul is always present.

- How can you tell the difference between the two? The voice of your soul always addresses you calmly, is always decisive and determined. The inner voice doesn't speak to your intellect, but to your feelings. Your inner being asks for attention by way of feelings, dreams, insights and passions.

- The trick is to allow all those feelings in without turning your daily life upside down. Living your daily life is the best way to practise hearing and recognizing your inner voice.

- Spirituality means listening to the voice of your soul, which will help you find your way in life. By finding and expressing your True Self, you will find happiness. Every person who does this, developing his or her own true nature, will make a positive difference in this world. And this has nothing to do with following spiritual 'rules', but with following your own inner compass.

- Living a spiritual life, being connected to your passion and life goal, is a matter of *not* suppressing your inner voice, but allowing it to be heard.

Afterword
SPIRITUALITY IS
NO 'SECRET'

*O*n the subject of what spirituality *is*, a lot more can be said. But I will stop here. This book will remain unfinished, just as I am, just as life will always be. There is no such thing as 'spiritual retirement'; there will not come a day when we can lean back and say: *So, now I pretty much know it all.* I do believe a day can come for every one of us when we can get up in the morning and say: *Yes, this is me, this is my life, and my life is an expression of who I really am.* Self-reflection, responsibility for ourselves, acceptance of ourselves and, most of all, surrendering to reality and letting go of our resistance to change – these offer us a context for living a deep, fulfilled and authentic life. I think I've covered a lot of ground on this subject in this book! I've given you tools that can help you move on – if that's what you want.

Is spirituality something complicated? The answer to this question is yes and no. It's complicated for those who want to keep believing in miracles from the outside, in some sort of magical salvation. It is simple for those who understand that life as we experience it is a reflection of our consciousness. It is not our circumstances that make life fascinating or give depth to our world, but the lenses of our consciousness through which we see that world. Or, as Schopenhauer said, 'Every man is pent up within the limits of his consciousness, and cannot directly get beyond those limits any more than he can get beyond his own skin.' It is our consciousness that determines if we can see beauty or love even in situations where people don't live up to our expectations. Our consciousness determines if we find peace even when our outside influences are chaotic. It determines whether we experience abundance or emptiness and whether we feel connected with everything living or lost in the maze of our own apartness.

◆

Just as a mother gives birth to her child,
we constantly give birth to new life.

◆

How can we become more conscious? By finding the true meaning in everything that appears on our path in life. By incorporating the outside world into our inner world. We suffer and struggle within ourselves if we see external circumstances as the cause of all that is lacking in our lives, all our sadness and pain. In fact, what we see in the outside world is usually nothing more than a symptom. Treating just those symptoms will keep us imprisoned in a consciousness vacuum, where we can't see that everything we experience as 'unwanted' or 'annoying' is the direct result of our inner contradictions. It is the universal law of creation: conflicts outside of you always point to a conflict inside of you; something is subconsciously working against what you consciously wish for yourself or others. So we become more conscious when we start to recognize what is the *cause* and what is the *effect*, learning to distinguish what is real from what is merely external appearance. You cannot develop your consciousness without taking on a personal confrontation with yourself.

Life develops from the inside out, not the other way around. Just as a mother gives birth to a child, we constantly give birth to new life by making new choices, taking a new view or cultivating a new mentality, by letting go of familiar thinking patterns and making room for fresh new feelings, thoughts and convictions. We discover more and more that this is how the process of creation works. That everything is creation. That we continuously create, whether we are conscious of it or not. We are willing participants in this universe, not just idle spectators; we are the co-creators of our existence. But be careful – no matter how hard we focus on a particular goal with our thoughts, no matter how strongly we visualize, it is highly unlikely that *anything* in our lives will change if something inside us doesn't change first. Change – nice sentence to put on your fridge – always starts on the inside. After that, the outside circumstances will follow suit. Developing self-knowledge and taking our own responsibility creates a connection to our inner fire and allows us to make well-thought-out use of the power of creation that we *are*.

•

We are willing participants in this universe, not just idle spectators; we are the co-creators of our existence.

•

This power of creation was not discovered by the authors of *The Secret*, nor does it belong to a few unique individuals on this planet; it is the power hidden in all of us. This power is no 'secret', hidden from the common folk for centuries. Each one of us has the power to shape our own existence. Everyone's life is what it is because it reflects what he or she believes to be true about life in that moment. Our relationships are the way they are because that's what we think we deserve. What we *are*, what we radiate, is what we attract. This is not news – it's just how creation works. Experience follows consciousness, not the other way around. Those who consciously and successfully shape their own lives and work with their own energy are doing one crucial thing: they are realizing their potential and following their hearts. They're tuned in to the voice deep inside of them and connected to their inner knowledge and strength.

The choice to live spiritually is, in its essence, a way to honour our True Self. That self is who we really are, instead of who we appear to be or think we should be. It is who we have always been and who we always will be. It is our universal core, which is as old as humanity itself. Once we realize our true strength and completely connect to our True Self, why would we ever fear or honour anything else?

Bibliography

Cools, Herman. *Het schitterende duister* (The Brilliant Darkness).
Haarlem: Altamira-Becht, 2007.

Hesse, Hermann. *Siddhartha*. London: Penguin Modern Classics, 2008.

Hillesum, Etty. *An Interrupted Life: The Diaries and Letters of Etty Hillesum*, 1941–1943. London: Persephone Books, 1999.

Kübler-Ross, Elisabeth. *The Wheel of Life: A Memoir of Living and Dying*.
London: Bantam Press, 1997.

Myss, Caroline. *Entering the Castle*. London: Simon & Schuster UK, 2007.

Postma, Annemarie. *Liefde maken* (Making Love). Amsterdam: Forum, 2007.

Postma, Annemarie. *The Deeper Secret*. London: Watkins Publishing, 2009.

Postma, Annemarie. *Vuile handen – stop de zeehondenjacht!* (Dirty Hands:
Stop the Seal Hunt!). Amsterdam: Arena, 2006.

Rubin, Harriet. *The Princessa: Machiavelli for Women*. London:
Bloomsbury, 1997.

Sathya Sai Baba newsletter, vol. 19, no. 1 (Spring 2004).

Sathya Sai Baba newsletter, vol. 19, no. 2 (Summer 2004).

Singer, Peter. *The Way We Eat: Why Our Food Choices Matter*. London:
Rodale, 2006.

Tolle, Eckhart. *The Power of Now*. London: Hodder and Stoughton, 2001.

Tulku Lama Lobsang. *108 Questions from the Secret Wisdom of Tibet*.
Vienna: Nangten Menlang International.

Walsch, Neale Donald. *Conversations with God, Book One*. London: Hodder
Mobius, 1997.

Williamson, Marianne. *The Age of Miracles*. London: Hay House UK, 2008.

Zukav, Gary. *The Seat of the Soul*. London: Rider, 1991.

Data on vegetarianism: www.vegsoc.org